GUIDELINES:
DEVELOPMENT OF NATIONAL PARKS AND PROTECTED AREAS FOR TOURISM

WORLD TOURISM ORGANIZATION

UNITED NATIONS ENVIRONMENT PROGRAMME

TERRESTRIAL ECOSYSTEMS BRANCH

INDUSTRY AND ENVIRONMENT PROGRAMME ACTIVITY CENTRE

c/ Capitán Haya, 42
28020 Madrid
Spain

Telephone: 34(1) 571 06 28
Fax: 34(1) 571 37 33
Telex: 42188 OMT E
Telegram: OMTOUR MADRID

Tour Mirabeau
39-43, quai André Citroën
75739 PARIS CEDEX 15
France

Telephone: 33(1) 40 58 88 50
Fax: 33(1) 40 58 88 74
Telex: 204 997 F
Telegram: UNITERRA PARIS

Prepared with the assistance of:
IUCN

**Jeffrey A. McNeely
James W. Thorsell
Héctor Ceballos-Lascuráin**

This is the first in a new series of joint publications on "Tourism and Environment" produced by WTO and UNEP. The series will include Guidelines, Technical Handbooks, Workshop or Seminar Proceedings and Studies undertaken by WTO and UNEP in pursuance of their Consultation and Co-operation Agreement of 1980. The series will also include publications prepared with the co-operation or assistance of other international organizations.

This "Tourism and Environment" technical series aims to meet the needs of a wide range of government officials, local communities, tourism industry managers and environment protection bodies, by providing information on the issues and methods of environmentally sustainable tourism development.

First edition: 1992

The designations employed and the presentation of the material in this publication do not imply the expression of any opinion whatsoever on the part of the World Tourism Organization or the United Nations Environment Programme concerning the legal status of any country, territory, city or area or of its authorities, or concerning delimitation of its frontiers or boundaries. Moreover, the views expressed do not necessarily represent the decision or the stated policy of the World Tourism Organization or the United Nations Environment Programme, nor does citing of trade names or commercial processes constitute endorsement.

WTO/UNEP JOINT PUBLICATION

Sales No. 92-III-D12

ISBN 92-844-0026-0

DISEÑO, MAQUETACION, FOTOMECANICA, FOTOCOMPOSICION
E IMPRESION: GRAFINORTE - TEL.: (91) 654 32 99. MADRID

GUIDELINES: DEVELOPMENT OF NATIONAL PARKS AND PROTECTED AREAS FOR TOURISM

TABLE OF CONTENTS

FOREWORD

Sustainable development requires part of the Earth's land area to be set aside as protected areas. Such areas, which include National Parks, make important contributions to human society by conserving the natural and cultural heritage for the enjoyment of people and ensuring ecological balance as nations' populations increase.

The upkeep of protected areas does, however, represent a substantial outlay, especially for developing countries. To recoup these costs many countries promote tourism in National Parks. Such a move not only recognizes the desire of people everywhere to seek solitude and contact with nature, but also offers them a chance to be acquainted with the natural heritage which they will hand on to future generations.

Tourism activity in a National Park or any other protected area can serve as a self-financing mechanism and hence as a tool of conservation. This will only be possible, however, if the level, type and management of tourism are appropriate and, in particular, the "carrying capacity" of the area is respected.

In order to assist countries to achieve sustainable stewardship of their National Parks and related protected areas, WTO and UNEP have joined forces to publish these Guidelines. They have been greatly assisted in their preparation by IUCN as consultant.

These Guidelines are a practical working document intended for use by all those concerned with management of National Parks and related protected areas. They can be used by:

- Managers of National Parks and their staff;

- Managers of related protected areas including parks established by state, provincial or regional authorities;

- Personnel of National Tourism Administrations responsible for planning, area development and siting of ecotourism attractions;

- Members of local committees in which parks or protected areas are sited.

It is hoped that all those who aim to ensure that tourism activity in National Parks supports conservation and respects the principle of sustainability will find these Guidelines a valuable and comprehensive reference for their work.

ACKNOWLEDGEMENTS

These Guidelines have been prepared by the World Tourism Organization (WTO) and the United Nations Environment Programme (UNEP) with the assistance of consultants from the International Union for the Conservation of Nature and Natural Resources (IUCN).

Section IV.4 has been entirely contributed by Professor Clare Gunn, Professor Emeritus, Texas A&M University, USA.

Valuable comments on earlier drafts have been received from a number of quarters, in particular from the Food and Agriculture Organization of the United Nations (FAO) which also contributed documentation to the project. The observations and suggestions of Gil Child, Michael Romeril and Stephen Halsey were greatly appreciated.

The original decision to prepare these Guidelines was taken by the WTO Environment Committee under the chairmanship of Mexico. The Guidelines were approved for publication by the Committee, under the chairmanship of the Netherlands, in May 1991.

UNEP staff participating in this project were:

Mrs M. Bjorklund, Senior Programme Officer, Wildlife and Protected Areas, Environmental Management

Mrs J. Aloisi de Larderel, Director, Industry and Environment Programme Activity Centre (IE/PAC)

Mrs H. Genot, Senior Consultant (IE/PAC)

WTO staff participating in this project were Peter Shackleford, Chief, Environment and Planning, with the assistance of Nicolai Kostiaev, Adrienne Boncy, Rosamond Deming and María Teresa Ortiz de Zárate.

IUCN staff participating in this project were Jeffrey A. McNeely, James W. Thorsell, Héctor Ceballos-Lascuráin.

(b)

(c)

Tourism to national parks and protected areas may be of domestic origin, as shown by these tourists taking a glass-bottom boat ride around the coral reefs near Koh Phi Phi Island, Thailand (a), or this local school group taken by bus to the Dryandra Forest Reserve in Western Australia (b). In other cases, such as Ngorongoro World Heritage Site, Tanzania (c) or Yosemite National Park, US (d), international tourism plays an important role.

Photos by Jeffrey A McNeely (a), Héctor Ceballos-Lascuráin (b) and (d), and James W Thorsell (c)

(d)

INTRODUCTION

1.   As human populations increase and the pressures of urban living encourage people to seek solitude with nature, the number of visitors to national parks and protected areas continues to rise. While most tourism to national parks has traditionally been domestic in origin, international tourism is also an important factor in such places as east and southern Africa, Costa Rica, India, Nepal, Indonesia, Australia and the U.S.

2.   Protected areas make important contributions to sustaining human society, especially through conserving the world's natural and cultural heritage. Values range from maintenance of representative samples of natural regions and preservation of biological diversity, to protecting the environmental stability of surrounding regions. Protected areas can provide opportunity

for rural development and rational use of marginal lands, for research and monitoring, for conservation, education, and for recreation and tourism. Consequently, over 130 countries have developed protected areas, which today cover nearly 5 percent of the land surface of the earth.

3.   Protected area systems vary considerably from one country to another, depending on needs and priorities, and on differences in legislative, institutional and financial support. Also, the range of services and values that protected areas provide is such that some management objectives are not compatible with others. This has lead to the establishment, by IUCN (International Union for Conservation of Nature and Natural Resources), of a system of protected area categories and definitions. Perhaps the best known of these categories is the National Park (Category II), of which some 1400 sites have been established, covering well over 300 million hectares (roughly the size of India).

(i) Tourism as a dynamic worldwide phenomenon

4.   Tourism has become one of the foremost economic activities around the world. It is estimated that in 1991 there were 449 million international arrivals in the world (WTO, 1992). In 1990 tourism generated 62.5 billion dollars for developing countries (WTO, 1991). Even travel and tourism to a highly developed country like the United States generates more foreign exchange than does exports of automobiles, agricultural goods or chemical products.

5.   Nature tourism, also known as ecotourism, is a relatively recent phenomenon, representing but one

(c)

(d)

weekend activity or an incidental part of a broader trip. For that reason, in this study the terms nature tourism and ecotourism are interchangeable.

(ii) Protected areas and national parks

6.   National parks are established to protect relatively large areas where:

(a) One or several ecosystems are not materially altered by human exploitation and occupation, where plant and animal species, geomorphological sites and habitats are of special scientific, educative and recreative interest or which contains a natural landscape of great beauty;

(b) the highest competent authority of the country has taken steps to prevent or eliminate as soon as possible exploitation or occupation in the whole area and to enforce effectively the respect of ecological, geomorphological, or aesthetic features which have led to its establishment; and

(c) visitors are allowed to enter, under special conditions, for inspirational,

*The diversity of ecotourism attractions: Basaseáchic Falls in the Sierra Madre of Chihuahua, Mexico (**a**), the millenary Drago tree (and endemic species) of Icod de los Vinos, Tenerife, Canary Islands (**b**), an elk foraging in Yellowstone National Park (**c**), a Laughing Kookaburra in Mount Coot-tha Reserve, near Brisbane, Australia (**d**), and the magnificent combination of rain forest and Classic Mayan architecture in Palenque, Chiapas, Mexico (**e**).*

Photos by Héctor Ceballos-Lascuráin

segment of the overall tourism industry. It is defined as tourism that involves traveling to relatively undisturbed natural areas with the specific object of studying, admiring and enjoying the scenery and its wild plants and animals, as well as any existing cultural aspects (both of the past or the present) found in these areas (Ceballos-Lascuráin, 1988). It is growing quickly, with one estimate putting 1988 earnings from nature tourism for developing countries at US$12 billion (Lindberg, 1991). Nature tourism is distinguished from mass tourism or resort tourism by having a lower impact on the environment and by requiring less infrastructure development. Ecotourism is a phenomenon composed of a wide spectrum of options, ranging from a hard-core, scientific approach to a casual visit to a natural area as a

(a)

(b)

(e)

educative, cultural and recreative purposes" (IUCN, 1990).

7.   National parks are, therefore, by definition available for public visitation. An international meeting held in New Delhi in November 1969 agreed that such use:

"could be combined with the primary function of nature conservation through a system of zoning. In this,

one zone would be established in which roads or other access ways may be constructed, buildings or other structures to accommodate tourism and park administrative functions may be located, and in which appropriate recreational facilities may be placed. This special tourism/administrative zone would not be one designated primarily for nature conservation, but would be so delimited and located as to create minimum interference with the nature conservation function of the park. National parks can also satisfy the public visitation function by establishing of wilderness areas over all or part of the national park, thus providing for limited tourism of a special kind" (IUCN, 1990).

8.   However, other categories of protected areas are also available for recreational and tourist use (see table 1 for a system of categories of protected areas); the differences rest in the management objectives for these areas, especially in the range of benefits they are designed to provide to local people. In this document the terms "national park" and "protected areas" are used interchangeably and are meant to describe natural areas that have some type of internationally accepted status of protection, and that also allow for at least some degree of visitation and tourism.

(iii) Purpose of the paper

9. A general statement on the role of tourism in protecting the environment has been prepared by WTO (1983) and a Joint Declaration on Tourism and the Environment has been signed with UNEP. In the context of these two documents, and in order to encourage more appropriate tourism development in national parks and protected areas, WTO and UNEP engaged IUCN to prepare guidelines which address:

-   ways and means of involving local people living in and around protected areas so that they may obtain increased social and economic benefits from tourism;

- determining what level of tourism is appropriate for a national park;

- improving the management of the natural values of the individual areas;

- designing appropriate tourism infrastructure in national parks;

- providing better educational and interpretive services to visitors;

- promoting greater appreciation by visitors of the values of national parks; and

- determining how the tourism activity in a national park can serve as a self-financing mechanism for the park and, hence, as a tool for conservation.

(iv) Orientation of the paper

10. The following guidelines are primarily oriented to national parks and protected areas in developing countries, hoping they will serve as a useful input in the establishment or revision of management plans for parks and protected areas in those countries.

Table 1. CATEGORIES AND MANAGEMENT OBJECTIVES OF PROTECTED AREAS

While all protected areas control human occupancy or use of resources to some extent, considerable latitude is available in the degree of such control. The following categories are arranged in ascending order of degree of human use permitted in the area.

I. **Scientific reserve/strict nature reserve**. To protect nature and maintain natural processes in an undisturbed state in order to have ecologically representative examples of the natural environment available for scientific study, environmental monitoring and education, and for the maintenance of genetic resources in a dynamic and evolutionary state.

II. **National park**. To protect outstanding natural and scenic areas of national or international significance for scientific, educational, and recreational use. These are relatively large natural areas not materially altered by human activity, and where commercial extractive uses are not permitted.

III. **Natural monument/natural landmark**. To protect and preserve nationally significant natural features because of their special interest or unique characteristics. These are relatively small areas focussed on protection of specific features.

IV. **Managed nature reserve/wildlife sanctuary**. To ensure the natural conditions necessary to protect nationally significant species, groups of species, biotic communities, or physical features of the environment when these require specific human manipulation for their perpetuation. Controlled harvesting of some resources may be permitted.

V. **Protected landscapes**. To maintain nationally significant natural landscapes characteristic of the harmonious interaction of man and land while providing opportunities for public enjoyment through recreation and tourism within the normal life-style and economic activity of these areas.

VI. **Resource reserve**. To protect the natural resources of the area for future use and prevent or contain development activities that could affect the resource pending the establishment of objectives based on appropriate knowledge and planning.

VII. **Natural biotic area/ anthropological reserve**. To allow the way of life of societies living in harmony with the environment to continue undisturbed by modern technology; resource extraction by indigenous people is conducted in a traditional manner.

VIII. **Multiple-use management area/managed resource.** To provide for the sustained production of water, timber, wildlife, pasture, and outdoor recreation, with the conservation of nature primarily oriented to the support of the economic activities (although specific zones can also be designed within these areas to achieve specific conservation objectives).

The Galápagos National Park of Ecuador is a good example of the major economic significance that may be attained by some protected areas in developing countries. (Paragraph 12)

Photo by Héctor Ceballos-Lascuráin

CHAPTER I

COSTS AND BENEFITS OF TOURISM IN PROTECTED AREAS

I.1 The role of tourism in national parks in developing countries

11. In addition to their many other functions (protecting watersheds and soils, ameliorating local climate, maintaining populations of important species of plants and animals, scientific research, education, improving environmental conditions in surrounding areas, and maintaining cultural values) national parks play an important role in promoting tourism in almost all developing countries. Many of these areas are focal points for international tourism, particularly in eastern and southern Africa, Costa Rica, Ecuador, India, Nepal, and Indonesia. In most countries of Asia and South America, tourism to national parks has primarily been a national phenomenon, and until very recently foreign tourism was only a secondary objective. Parks such as Iguazu in Brazil and Argentina receive over 2 million visitors a year, most from nearby cities. Cibodas Reserve in Java, Khao Yai National Park in Thailand, Bharatpur National Park in India are other examples where domestic tourism and recreation is very significant.

I.2 Economics of tourism in national parks

12. Tourism to natural areas is economically important in many developing countries; in virtually all tropical areas, the attractions of nature are used in tourist promotions irrespective of whether national parks are appropriately developed for tourism. In the countries with particularly outstanding natural attractions, tourism is often used as the primary justification for the creation of national parks. In Kenya, for example, tourism is the largest earner of foreign currency, and contributed $400 million in foreign exchange in 1988. In Rwanda's Parc National des Volcans, tourists going to see the gorillas generate annually about $ 1 million in entrance fees, and $2 to $3 million in other expenditures. Nepal earned about $45 million in 1983 from visitors attracted primarily by Himalayan geography, nature, and culture. The Galápagos National Park of Ecuador earns direct tourism revenues of at least $700,000 a year, with a potential of earning well over $25 million per year (Lindberg 1991). Economic models in Kenya's Amboseli National Park showed each lion to be worth $27,000/year in tourism revenues; the elephant herd was determined to be worth about $610,000/year merely for viewing purposes. Such animals are worth far more alive as a tourist attraction than dead; the comparable gross yield from hunting would be appreciably less than 10% of this value. Moreover, the total park net returns (due mainly to tourism) amount to $40 per hectare a year compared to 80 cents per hectare under

the most optimistic agricultural returns (Western, 1982).

13. Among conservation officers in East Africa, the often voiced principle is "Wildlife pays, so wildlife stays". But nature tourism in developed countries is an even more lucrative business. The U.S. National Park System, for example, is by far the largest single system of travel attraction anywhere in the world, having received over 270 million visitors in 1989 (Baker, 1990); and state parks (those managed by the state government rather than the U.S. federal government) draw over 500 million visitors, with many states showing annual attendance of over five times the total population of the state. In Canada, national parks draw over 20 million visitors annually, with the provincial parks drawing an additional 47 million per year (Prescott-Allen and Prescott-Allen, 1986).

14. In 1985, a total of 167.5 million U.S. citizens 16 years of age and older participated in some kind of wildlife-associated recreation, including both consumptive (hunting and fishing) and nonconsumptive activities (U.S. Fish and Wildlife Service, 1988). The latter activities greatly outnumbered the consumptive ones: 161 million people engaged in at least one type of nonconsumptive activity, versus 50.6 million individuals who fished and 18.5 million who hunted. Nonconsumptive expenditures of Americans 16 years of age and older were $14 billion, of which

The US National Parks System (exemplified here by Yellowstone National Park) is the largest single system of travel attractions anywhere in the world.

Photo by Héctor Ceballos-Lascuráin

$4.4 billion were trip-related. In addition to the national and state park figures quoted above, some 29.5 million Americans 16 years old and older took trips primarily to observe, photograph, or feed wildlife. As the largest single category, birdwatching provided primary non-residential enjoyment for 25 million people. The 29.5 million travelers were engaged in 274 million trips away from their place of residence, including 1,130,000 U.S. citizens who went abroad in 1985 for nature tourism purposes, spending a total of more than 8 million days abroad. At an average of US$100 per day spent by each American in a foreign country during his

Birdwatchers, like these shown in Perth, Australia (a), constitute the largest single category of persons involved in some kind of non-consumptive wildlife-associated recreation. They are attracted by birds as diverse as the Turquoise-browed motmot, found in tropical Middle America (b), the tawny frogmouth of Australia (c) or the widespread osprey, shown here at its nest in Baja California (d).

Photos by Héctor Ceballos-Lascuráin

(b)

(c)

(d)

ecotourism trip, this means an expenditure of over $800 million for all foreign countries visited by American nature tourists in 1985.

15. The socio-economic benefits of tourism in national parks can be considerable. This study is not the place for a detailed analysis of these benefits (see Lindberg, 1991 and Boo, 1990 for more details), but at least the following can be noted:

- Tourism generates local employment, both directly in the tourism sector and in the various support and resource management sectors;

- It stimulates profitable domestic industries — hotels, restaurants, transport systems, souvenirs and handicrafts and guide services;

- It generates foreign exchange;

- It diversifies the local economy, particularly in rural areas where agricultural employment may be sporadic or insufficient;

- It stimulates the rural economy by creating demand for agricultural produce and injecting capital;

- It stimulates improvements to local transportation and communications infrastructures, which brings benefits to local people;

- Since protected areas which are developed for tourism become showpiece areas of a country, local government may be willing to provide extra resources to promote development in surrounding areas;

- It encourages productive use of lands which are marginal for agriculture, enabling large tracts of land to remain covered in natural vegetation;

- It improves intercultural understanding and global communication;

- If adequately conducted, it can provide a self-financing mechanism for the park authorities and consequently serve as a tool for conservation of the natural heritage.

- It creates recreational facilities which can be used by local communities as well as domestic and foreign visitors; and

- It prompts conservation by convincing government officials and the general public of the importance of natural areas.

16. These benefits are particularly relevant where the land allocated for the protected area has little or no value for agriculture. The benefits will become ever more valuable as the availability of other wild recreation areas is further reduced. Moreover, properly planned and managed tourism — which is what ecotourism is really about — is both non-polluting and renewable.

17. If ecotourism is to receive a higher priority in government plans, especially in developing countries, considerable effort must be made to effectively involve local inhabitants in the tourism activity. Usually, the rural populations living closest to protected areas are characterized by very low incomes, with few viable economic options. Ecotourism can represent for these people a valid economic alternative, with the additional advantage that these inhabitants can be converted into the most efficient wardens and conservationists of these natural areas, since their welfare depends on the preservation of the natural qualities of their environment. Frequently, these local inhabitants possess a notable practical and ancestral knowledge of the natural features of their region (landscape, flora and fauna) and — with a certain amount of training — can be developed into effective nature guides. They can also directly participate in economic activities derived from the operation of hotels, restaurants and other tourism services. In many cases, local community organizations can act as concessionaires of tourism services,

with appropriate administrative training (Ceballos-Lascuráin, 1990).

I.3 Concessions

18. Usually, protected area management authorities, especially in the less developed countries, lack the technical, economical, and organisational resources required to effectively manage and develop tourism activities in their protected areas. In most cases, it is more appropriate for the park authorities to rent concessions for specific individuals, firms, or local communities for specific tourism activities, such as building and operating lodges, restaurants, or curio shops; horse-back riding, boat excursions, and other forms of transport; guided hiking or bird-watching

Local inhabitants possess a notable practical and ancestral knowledge of the natural features of their region and -with a certain amount of training- can be developed into effective nature guides like these sherpas in Chitwan National Park, Nepal (a) or this gaucho at the Quebrada de los Cuervos Nature Reserve in Uruguay (b).

Photos by Jeffrey A. McNeely (a) and Héctor Ceballos-Lascuráin (b)

(a)

(b)

9

Different examples of concessions in protected areas: Yellowstone Lodge in Yellowstone National Park (a), swimming pool facilities in Niokolo Koba National Park, Senegal (b), tour boat in Fiordland National Park in New Zealand (c), local people selling souvenirs in Ao Phang Nga National Park, Thailand (d).

Photos by Héctor Ceballos-Lascuráin (a) and (b), James W. Thorsell (c) and Jeffrey A. McNeely (d)

tours; souvenirs, book shops, field guides; and the many other goods and services required to support tourism. Of course, this implies having a sound management plan for the park in question and also the need for the park authorities to enforce the guidelines and rules set forth (see Chapter IV, below). Through the use of concessions, local people can reap benefits from nature tourism and they will eventually be the best guardians of the park, since their livelihood is at stake. Concessions can also contribute, along with entrance fees, to the self-financing mechanisms so badly needed by protected areas affected by shrinking government budgets.

I.4 Social and economic benefits of tourism in marine parks

19.   Scuba diving, snorkeling, swimming, surfing and sunbathing bring tourists to small nations frequently with little else to offer people. For example, the natural beauty of the Seychelles Islands, the coral sand beaches, the reefs and the rich natural history are that country's major drawing card for tourists. Each year millions of North Americans, Japanese, and Europeans visit the Caribbean and Pacific islands, the Mediterranean coasts and Florida beaches to relax in the sun at the water's edge, to dive over wrecks and reefs, to sail and water-ski, to fish and to enjoy seafood. Tourism is a major industry in these areas from which many countries are gaining jobs, revenue, and foreign exchange. Therefore, protected areas, with adequate management plans, should be incorporated into the national plan for tourism development in coastal countries. Marine parks not only arouse interest but, properly managed, also help to maintain the quality of recreation resources that attract tourists.

20.   Significant benefits have become evident in several places where the coral reefs have been protected including the following sites: the Netherlands Antilles (Bonaire Marine Park), where diving tourism has increased; the Seychelles (Ste. Anne

National Marine Park), where the park is used by both residents and tourists for swimming, sailing, snorkelling, diving and glass-bottom boat excursions; Fiji (Tai Island), where subsistence catches have increased, tourist activity has expanded and the holders of traditional fishing rights are involved in resort management and boat hire; Cozumel Island (Mexican Caribbean), where increasing numbers of foreign and national tourists are coming to observe the coral-dwelling fish; and Kenya (Malindi/Watamu National Parks and Reserves), where tourism generates revenues through gate, guide and camping fees, rental of boats and equipment and hotel expenses. It also has indirect benefits through the creation of jobs in hotels and for guides and boatmen.

(d)

21. A number of parameters may be used to measure monetary benefits of protecting coastal and marine areas, including:

- gate or license fee totals to estimate the economic value of tourism to the protected area; these are also indicators of the willingness of the public to pay for recreation privilege at the site;

- total tonnage at dockside or retail value landings to calculate the contribution of a protected area to linked fishery revenues (i.e. the economic value of the breeding ground of a fishery resource);

- total income from recreational and commercial equipment, lodgings, food and transportation to estimate the contribution of a protected area to linked supportive industries;

- total hotel catering, product processing and packaging, equipment production (factory) and distribution (outlet), guide, and other jobs in industries linked to the protected area.

- the probable total cost of property damage (to roads, buildings, livestock and crops) through storm waves and winds multiplied by the probability of storm damage (i.e.

after the felling of mangroves, disturbance of dune vegetation or the blasting of coral reefs) to obtain an estimate of the annual benefit of natural storm damage control.

- as stated by Hufschmidt *et al.*, (1983), "Conservation of natural systems will, to some extent, necessarily be rationalised on the basis of social objectives that cannot be quantified and monetised". Examples of these follow:

- the number of students or student groups, the range in ages, and the number of teaching institutions represented to give estimates of the value of the protected area to education, particularly if before and after counts are available to indicate how protection has directly benefitted education;

- the number of researchers, research projects, theses and publications to estimate the value of the protected area to research; and

- head, bus, boat or group counts of visitors to a protected area to calculate the extent of use. Expressed as a total or a percentage of the state or national population, this gives an estimate of the social value of the site.

(a)

(b)

*The observation of coral-dwelling fish in Xel-há, in the Mexican Caribbean, has become a popular activity for national and foreign tourists (**a**). Tulum National Park, also in the Mexican Caribbean, is an important tourist attraction because it combines interesting Maya ruins, lowland tropical forest, a spectacular coastline and crystal-clear waters (**b**).*

Photos by Héctor Ceballos-Lascuráin

I.5 Negative impacts of tourism on national parks

22.   Even though protected, national parks are not immune to deterioration as a result of inappropriate management, pressure from the surrounding human population, and over-use by tourists. One of the most pressing problems of many national parks and protected areas today is how to cope with the increasing number of visitors seeking recreation in natural environments.

23.   Many of the places visited by ecotourists support fragile ecosystems which cannot endure heavy disturbances. The original management plan for the Galápagos National Park, for example, called for a maximun of 12,000 visitors. The actual number of visitors has gone from 7,500 in 1975 to 32,595

in 1987 (Lindberg, 1991) and many researchers are now concerned that this excessive and uncontrolled flow may be causing severe environmental degradation.

24.   In some instances, tourism negatively affects the wildlife in protected areas. Cheetahs and lions, for example, have been reported to decrease their hunting activity when surrounded by more than six vehicles (Western and Henry, 1979). In both Annapurna and Sagarmatha, trekkers are utilising the natural resources available in an unsustainable way. Tree cutting for firewood has caused serious environmental deterioration.

25.   Other potential negative impacts which may be noted include:

- Local people may come to view protected areas as being established for the benefit of foreigners rather than for themselves. Other socio-cultural impacts have been well documented by the University of the South Pacific (1980);

- Many areas of important conservation value have very little appeal to tourists (e.g., extensive tracts of tropical forest and most mangrove swamps), so they may receive inadequate attention from the management agency;

- If decision-makers are led to believe that parks exist primarily for economic gain, and their expectations in this direction are not fulfilled, they may begin to look for more profitable alternative uses for the land; and

- Governments may attempt to seek to maximize economic returns from parks through inappropriate developments, but large hotels, highways or golf courses designed to attract more visitors can diminish a park's natural values and eventually turn it into an area for which the main objective is mass tourism rather than conservation.

I.6 Balance of positive and negative impacts

26. The benefits of tourism in national parks can be considerable, but the adverse effects which inevitably accompany the positive ones need to be addressed by careful planning and effective management.

27. The guiding principle for tourism development in national parks is to manage the natural and human resources so as to maximize visitor enjoyment while minimizing negative impacts of tourism development. This requires an objective assessment of potential negative impacts and a thoughtful analysis of how this potential can be controlled. Mistakes have been made in developing tourism in protected areas worldwide and the resulting damage is all too evident. Table 2 provides a checklist of a number of real or potential negative impacts of tourism.

Careful monitoring of the number of tourist vehicles which approach species such as lions is necessary to avoid disturbance. In the photo, visitors to Kenya's Amboseli National Park.

Photo by James W. Thorsell

Rapid growth of international tourist demand at Lugano, Switzerland (a) and Cancún, Mexico (b), has required careful planning to avoid overdevelopment.

Photo by Jeffrey A. McNeely (a) and Héctor Ceballos-Lascuráin (b)

(b)

(a)

TABLE 2. POTENTIAL ENVIRONMENTAL EFFECTS OF TOURISM IN PROTECTED AREAS: THE TYPES OF NEGATIVE VISITOR IMPACTS THAT MUST BE CONTROLLED

Factor Involved	Impact on Natural Quality	Comment
Overcrowding	Environmental stress, animals show changes in behaviour	Irritation, reduction in quality, need for carrying-capacity limits or better regulation
Overdevelopment	Development of rural slums, excessive manmade structures	Unsightly urban-like development
Recreation:		
Powerboats	Disturbance of wildlife	Vulnerability during nesting seasons, noise pollution
Fishing	None	Competition with natural predators
Foot safaris	Disturbance of wildlife	Overuse and trail erosion
Pollution:		
Noise (radios, etc.)	Disturbance of natural sounds	Irritation to wildlife and other visitors
Litter	Impairment of natural scene, habituation of wildlife to garbage	Aesthetic and health hazard
Vandalism destruction	Mutilation and facility damage	Removal of natural features
Feeding of wildlife	Behavioural changes danger to tourists	Removal of habituated animals
Vehicles:		
Speeding	Wildlife mortality	Ecological changes, dust
Off-road driving	Soil and vegetation damage	Disturbance to wildlife
Miscellaneous:		
Souvenir collection	Removal of natural attractions, disruptions of natural processes	Shells, coral, horns, trophies, rare plants
Firewood	Small wildlife mortality habitat destruction	Interference with natural energy flow
Roads and excavations	Habitat loss, drainage	Aesthetic scars
Power lines	Destruction of vegetation	Aesthetic impacts
Artificial water holes and salt provision	Unnatural wildlife concentrations, vegetation damage	Replacement of soil required
Introduction of exotic plants and animals	Competition with wild species	Public confusion

(Adapted from Thorsell, 1984)

CHAPTER II

TOURISM CONSIDERATIONS IN SELECTION OF AREAS FOR NATIONAL PARKS

II.1 Potential for tourism

28.   In many countries tourism plays a major role in the establishment of protected areas and an area's "tourist potential" is an important factor in the selection process. Some of the factors which make an area attractive to visitors are indicated in the checklist provided in Table 3. Growing numbers of vacationers seek recreation in a warm tropical country; they want to see something different, something new, something spectacular, something to photograph; sometimes they want to travel in comfort, with minimal effort; and many times they want to mix their "adventure" with leisure activities such as sunbathing, swimming and shopping.

29.   Consequently the most successful tourist packages combine a number of different interests — sport, wildlife, local customs, historical sites, spectacular scenes, food and dancing and, most of all, water. The sea, lakes, rivers, swimming pools and waterfalls all have high recreation value, particularly for domestic tourism.

30.   However, and this is a very recent trend, growing numbers of people from the more developed countries are showing an interest in specialized tours that are oriented towards "exotic" natural and cultural features, found mainly in developing countries. This striking phenomenon is chanelling greater numbers of visitors to hitherto unvisited parks such as Sagarmatha (Nepal), Komodo Island (Indonesia), Manu (Perú), Galápagos Islands (Ecuador), Iguazú Falls (Brazil-Argentina), and the Grey Whale Sanctuaries in Baja California (México).

31.   Tourist potential in protected areas frequently drops off fast, however, as the expense, time and discomfort of travel increases or when danger is involved in access to the tourist destination. Nairobi National Park receives the most visitors of any park in Kenya, because it is the park closest to the capital and easiest for visitors to reach. The variety and close proximity of natural habitats protected by Costa Rica's park system has made that country extremely popular for nature tourism groups.

32.   Wildlife as a large-scale tourist attraction in Africa and parts of Asia is also a delicate matter. Certain animals

such as lions, leopards, tigers, elephants, rhinos and gorillas have big visitor appeal but other wildlife, just as fascinating to the scientist, seems to have lower "star" quality. Reliability of sighting is also necessary. It is not enough to know you have a chance to see a tiger — visitors want to have a reasonable guarantee that they will see a tiger before they come in any substantial numbers.

33. Moreover, some visitors may be "spoiled" by the quality of wildlife television films and the quality of viewing in the really top parks and tend not to be satisfied with less spectacular reserves. One solution is, of course, to employ good knowledgeable guides — preferably local ones — to make wildlife viewing as interesting and rewarding as possible but even so certain habitats are easier of access and more open for viewing game.

34. Tropical rainforests, which on first sight may surprisingly appear to be devoid of wildlife to many visitors, can be made more interesting with imaginative presentation: aerial walkways, board walks, observation towers, interpretive centers, indigenous people as guides, river-running (e.g., in Borneo), hides for wildlife viewing. This is required if they are to compete with African savannas in terms of interesting wildlife or the Himalayas for the spectacular scenery.

35. The role of protected area management in providing tourist objectives and facilities must be developed in close coordination with the regional and national tourist authority. The tourist board may sometimes even provide financial assistance for developing tourist facilities in reserves. Managers of protected areas must also explain to the tourist authorities what limits the respective protected areas must place on visitor use so that carrying capacities are not exceeded. Unless carefully controlled, the volume of visitors may have a deleterious impact on parks and eventually destroy the very resource on which tourism depends. In Kenya's Amboseli National Park, for instance, heavy visitor traffic concentrated in a small area and numerous vehicles located round a single predator have resulted in severe stress on sensitive species such as cheetah, unnecessary habitat destruction and deteriorating visitor satisfaction (Govt. of Kenya, 1981). Similarly the Government of Nepal's restrictions on expeditions to their mountain parks have been an attempt to regulate use in a high impact setting.

TABLE 3. CHECKLIST ON TOURISM POTENTIAL OF PROTECTED AREAS

Is the protected area: - close to an international airport or major tourist centre? - moderately close? - remote?	**Does the area have additional:** - high cultural interest? - some cultural attractions? - few cultural attractions?
Is the journey to the area: - easy and comfortable? - a bit of an effort? - arduous or dangerous?	**Is the area:** - unique in its appeals? - a little bit different? - similar to other visitor reserves?
Does the area offer the following: - 'star' species attractions? - other interesting wildlife? - representative wildlife? - distinctive wildlife viewing, e.g. on foot, by boat, from hides?	**Does the area have:** - a beach or lakeside recreation facilities? - river, falls or swimming pools? - no other recreation?
Is successful wildlife viewing: - guaranteed? - usual? - with luck or highly seasonal?	**Is the area close enough to other sites of tourist interest to be part of a tourist circuit?** - yes, other attractive sites - moderate potential - low or no such potential
Does the area offer: - several distinct features of interest? - more than one feature of interest ? - one main feature of interest?	**Is the surrounding area:** - of high scenic beauty or intrinsic interest? - quite attractive? - rather ordinary?
What standards of food and accommodation are offered? - high standards; - adequate standards; - rough standards	

Source: MacKinnon et al., 1987

CHAPTER III

LIMITS TO USE: TOURISM CARRYING CAPACITY

INTRODUCTION

36.   Once the selection of sites for national parks has been determined, it is necessary to estimate the capacity of those areas to absorb visitors so that such use is sustainable. WTO, UNEP and others have devoted much attention to this topic (see Tourism and Environment.   WTO/UNEP Joint Technical Report Series, 1992, "Tourism Carrying Capacity"), and we offer here a general summary of the principal parameters involved in determining capacity levels.

III.1 Definition of carrying capacity

37.   "Carrying capacity" is the level of visitor use an area can accommodate with high levels of satisfaction for visitors and few impacts on resources. The concept implies that there are limits to visitor use. Carrying capacity estimates are determined by many factors; in the end, they depend on administrative decisions about approximate sustainable levels of use. The major factors in estimating carrying capacity are (a) environmental, (b) social, and (c) managerial.

38.   Boullón (1985) offers a formula to estimate the tourist carrying capacity of a given area, which consists of dividing the area to be used by tourists by the average individual "standard" (usually in m2/person) required. This individual standard, however, is not easily arrived at, and must be carefully defined for each particular case, since it involves at least three capacity variables: material; psychological; and ecological. Once this average standard has been specifically determined for each particular area (having in mind also the different activities nature tourists are involved in), then:

$$\text{Carrying capacity} = \frac{\text{Area used by tourists}}{\text{Average individual standard}}$$

The total number of allowed daily visits is then obtained:

Total of daily visits = Carrying capacity x Rotation coefficient

Where the rotation coefficient is determined thus:

$$\text{Rotation coefficient} = \frac{\text{N}^{\circ} \text{ of daily hours area is open for tourists}}{\text{Average time of visit}}$$

39. Environmental factors to consider in determining carrying capacity include the following:

- Size of area and usable space. Iguazú National Park, Brazil, for example, has 170,000 hectares but only a small portion is accessible.

- Fragility of environment. Some areas have very fragile soils or other features vulnerable to use (e.g. sand dune vegetation, alpine zones).

- Wildlife resources. Carrying capacity is affected by numbers, diversity, and distribution of wildlife. Record dry and wet season patterns, availability of highly attractive species, and their concentration areas.

- Topography and vegetative cover. Rolling bush country can conceal or buffer visitors. In flat grassland, visitor vehicles are highly visible, reducing carrying capacity.

- Specific behavioural sensitivity of certain animal species to human visitation. This has to be determined by biologists versed in the ethology of the involved species. For example, regarding gorilla tourism in Uganda, a maximum of 4 visitors per troop per day was established in 1989 during the pilot phase of a project to restore and develop gorilla tourism in that country (Uganda Tourism Development Report, 1990).

40. Social factors to consider when determining carrying capacity include the following:

- Viewing pattern. Is it evenly distributed or concentrated? (In Amboseli National Park, Kenya, for example, 90% of use occurs in 10% of the area, 50% of use between the hours of 15.30 and 18.30).

- Tourists' viewing choices. If viewing is largely of a few attractions, crowding is more likely. (Amboseli is heavily congested around its three prides of lions).

- Visitors' opinions. How do visitors rate the park at present use levels? What are their opinions about crowding?

- Availability of facilities. Number of lodge beds and campsites is a controlling factor.

41. A number of management procedures can be used to increase carrying capacity:

- design viewing tracks, trails, etc., to distribute use widely;

- reduce conflict between competing uses (e.g. zone area for special campsites or hotels);

- provide adequate information and interpretation services;

- increase durability of heavily used resources (e.g. surfacing materials).

- provide facilities and design policies that encourage wet or off-season use.

III.2 Carrying capacity for tourism on islands

42. Despite the large capital infrastructure needed, and the environmental change that mass tourism brings wherever it becomes established, it is notable that tourist entrepreneurs are seldom required by governments to produce either social or environmental impact assessments of the results of importing large numbers of people into islands (or elsewhere) under tourist development schemes. Changes brought by tourism may be lamented or admired retrospectively, but few attempts are made to anticipate them, so that the "carrying capacity" of fragile insular ecosystems can be defined in terms of tourist numbers, duration of stay or mode of behaviour. Package tourists, who travel in busloads from airport to motel to enjoyment sites, have different environmental impacts than small parties of independent hikers. The management and development of national parks demands some census and assessment of the environmental

impacts of such different types of visitors. The same impact assessments need to be made of tourists to islands as an important information base in defining their tourist carrying capacities and thus protecting island habitats (see MacEachern and Towle, 1974).

The carrying capacity of fragile insular ecosystems must be carefully determined, as when it was planned to install a cablecar leading to the summit of Teide Volcano in Teide National Park, Tenerife, Canary Islands.

Photo by Héctor Ceballos-Lascuráin

CHAPTER IV

PLANNING FOR TOURISM IN NATIONAL PARKS

IV.1 Management planning

43. Ideally, every national park should have a management plan which guides all developments within the park and defines the objectives of the park in terms of the wider region. Planning specifically for touristic uses in a national park is one part of the overall park management planning process. Under IUCN's standardized approach which has been adopted by many tropical countries, the park management plan addresses four main elements that make up management:

- resource management and protection
- human use (including tourism)
- research and monitoring
- administration

44. Within the context of the total management planning process the human use or tourism "sub-programme" would address a number of specific concerns as outlined below. The steps in preparing the tourism part of the plan are summarized as follows:

45. **Step 1. Collect and Analyze Data**. To ensure that decisions are based on a thorough understanding of local resources, social and economic factors, and other considerations, data on a wide range of relevant parameters should be collected and analyzed systematically by the national park authority.

46. Tourism means managing people and it is thus necessary to be familiar with the human side of the equation. It is important to gather information on an area's visitors, just as it is important to monitor natural resources. Visitor information is required for (a) budgeting and setting fees, (b) allocating personnel, (c) scheduling maintenance, (d) understanding the users, (e) detecting trends in use, and (f) planning.

47. Sorts of tourism data which should be collected by park managers include:

- Basic entry figures should be collected to indicate the number of visitors, by entry gate and arrival mode (air, automobile, or bus).

- Travel patterns and visitor activities (viewing, camping, picnicking, walking, fishing, education, etc.).

- Periods of use so that peak periods can be accommodated.

- Visitors' places of origin, to clarify the market area and the staff's language requirements.

- Visitors' lengths of stay.

- Levels of visitor satisfaction and suggestions for improvements.

48. **Step 2. Identify Resource Conflicts.** On the basis of resource inventories and other data collected under Guideline 1, the management authority should identify resource conflicts and define options for solving such conflicts (including costs and benefits of each option).

49. Conflicts between resource use for tourism and for the livelihood of local inhabitants need to be anticipated. The national parks authority should create mechanisms to harmonize the development of resources and, wherever possible, blend tourist development with the local culture and way of life. For tourism developments in coastal and island habitats, the following potential resource conflicts are indicative of the type of issue that a tourism planner would face:

- **Fishing.** Fishing at a subsistence or modest market level in a specific locality may have evolved a balance between supply and off-take over a number of years. With the greatly increased demand that may be stimulated by major tourist developments, the traditional fishery may be forced out of balance with the available resource. This can quickly lead to over-fishing, rising prices, and a reduced protein supply for the local population. Therefore, as part of every tourism development plan, improved fisheries management procedures should be implemented. These would include steps such as a

system for reporting catch data to determine stock levels; protection of nursery areas by preventing habitat destruction, and by prohibiting fishing where necessary; establishment and enforcement of standards for net or seine mesh size adequate to protect juveniles and non-selected smaller fish; and establishment of specific "replenishment zones" where no fishing is permitted (such a zone should include the best available coral reefs and could be combined with development for fish observation by tourists using glass-bottom boats or snorkels).

- **Mangroves.** Mangrove ecosystems play a key role as feeding and spawning areas for a great number of commercially-important fish and other marine animals. They help regulate the movement of fresh and salt water in the intertidal zone and provide a habitat for a wide range of species. Their protection is essential for the maintenance of the productivity of coastal waters. Appropriate national policies on environment, management and conservation of mangrove have been established and should be followed by any tourism development plan.

- **Unique sites.** Management of unique sites is urgent where facilities for tourists and accompanying local settlement endanger the natural site. Privately financed development often actively seeks hotel locations as near as possible to outstandingly beautiful and unique coastal land forms and beach areas. Therefore, development should be preceded by an inventory and a zoning/management plan to ensure preservation and public use of valuable natural sites, especially where there may be a high demand on coastal lands for recreational use, or where outstanding attractions are found close to existing high-density tourist facilities.

- **Sites of outstanding natural values.** Some areas of naturally

In order to avoid conflicts between resource use for tourism and for the local inhabitants, careful surveys must be carried out. Here, park professionals exchange ideas with dwellers in Chitwan National Park, Nepal.

Photo by Jeffrey A. McNeely

high primary productivity — such as wetlands, seagrass beds, coral reefs, and mature rainforests — should receive high priority for preservation or protective management. Wherever destruction or serious alteration is contemplated, benefits and costs should be carefully assessed. Features with unusual aesthetic value may be important to an existing or potential tourist industry, so developments in a tourist zone may well help to support the establishment or improved management of a nearby national park; in coastal habitats, the most critical reef ecosystems should be given special status, such as Marine Park, and supervision and law enforcement should be provided.

50.   **Step 3. Determine Objectives.** The national parks authority should determine, through discussion and negotiation with those most directly concerned, detailed and appropriate objectives for each tourist zone.

51.   Deciding objectives is the most important step in determining what sort of tourism facilities are appropriate to a tourist zone; all else follows from the decisions made on objectives. When objectives are only implicit, their full implications may not be appreciated and different parties may have different perceptions of the objectives. Therefore, objectives must be made explicitly and since such decisions will almost always involve value judgements, they should be finally decided at an appropriately high level after having been thoroughly discussed by a wide range of interests. At least the following categories of objectives should be considered:

-    **Beneficiaries.** Who are to be the primary beneficiaries? Options may include: (1) the local people (they should have the highest priority); (2) foreign investors (i.e., bringing capital from outside the country in varying degrees); (3) tourist agencies; (4) major national investors from outside the zone (e.g., from the capital). The sort of development promoted will vary widely with the intended beneficiary,

but the primary beneficiaries may also become the most dependent on the tourism resource.

-    **Dependency.** To what extent should the area become dependent on tourism, realizing that the supply of tourists is uncertain and dependent on a wide range of factors over which the park agency has no control? Options may include: (1) tourism should become the mainstay of the local economy, and involve the local people to the maximum extent; (2) tourism should be a useful supplement to the local people, but they should be primarily dependent on their traditional livelihood (e.g., agriculture or fishing); (3) local people should be minimally involved in the development, instead bringing labor from distant urban centers (this option may be considered when governments have determined that the local culture would be significantly damaged by contact with tourists, as might be the case in some Amazonian protected areas). The social, economic, and environmental consequences of these three sorts of options will vary widely.

-    **Scale.** Based partly on questions of beneficiaries and dependency, what scale of tourism should be promoted? There should be an explicit statement, included as an integral feature of the plan for the Tourist Zone, of the level at which further growth of tourism would be limited and how this would be done. Maintenance of the quality of life in any small island or coastal setting requires the fixing of carrying capacity ceilings; these will vary with the fragility of the area concerned and the nature of the tourist activity contemplated.
    In striking the balance among beneficiaries, dependency, and scale, full weight should always be given to the effect on the social fabric of local communities brought about by the promotion of mass tourism. These include impacts associated with a change in the

consumption and behavior patterns of local people through exposure to ideas and life styles of tourists. Local people should be protected from decisions made by certain developers who may have a short-term vested interest in rapid expansion and increase in land values through speculation, and may not be overly concerned by the possibility that the tourism engendered may be of a quite ephemeral nature.

Source. What sources of tourism should be given priority? Options may include: (1) primarily local (with one implication being that while the economic scale may be somewhat less, the supply is likely to be more dependable); (2) primarily foreign (with the implication that while economic benefits — especially in terms of foreign exchange — may be higher, there is more uncertainty in supply). If the intention is to address primarily the foreign market, then the specific sector of that market needs to be decided and developments designed to address the interests of that sector (options may vary from retired Japanese businessmen to Australian back-packers).

52. International tourism, by definition, draws persons from diverse cultures. Regional resource inventories and evaluations for the development of tourism should therefore attempt to take into account diverse recreational preferences. The travel preferences of tourists from different cultures (or groups within cultures) should also be considered in the layout and design of tourist facilities. For large tourist zones, a wide range of different interests can be met by different sorts of lodging and other facilities. For long-term security the bottom line is the development of local support and therefore benefits to the immediate region of all tourism projects should be maximized.

53. **Step 4. Fit Tourism into Regional Context.** Because of its interaction with other land-use activities pursued in islands or coastal areas under development, the planning and promotion of tourism should be undertaken at the highest government levels and viewed as a component part of an integrated, comprehensive resource management plan founded on sound ecological principles.

54. All national parks should be integrated with the general land use plan for the region. Similarly, plans for specific tourism developments within a given park should be coordinated with other land-use plans, both locally and regionally. The overall land-use plan for a region should consider the economic benefits that will accrue to the region from tourism developments in the tourist zone. These benefits should be balanced against possible developments outside the zone which could have deleterious efforts on the attractiveness of the tourist zone. Where expansion of the tourist sector is planned, a commensurate expansion of public services should be mandatory; this will usually require collaboration among a wide range of government and private institutions.

55. **Step 5. Prepare Management Plan.** The national parks authority should formulate a plan for each tourist zone in coordination with other government agencies and the local government, covering specifically those aspects pertaining to tourism. The tourism subprogramme of the management plan is to be fully coordinated and integrated with other sectoral plans for the area. The plan should include a zoning plan and specify the sorts of activities which are permissible in each zone, based on the objectives agreed following Step 3.

56. The infrastructure of the tourist industry can eventually destroy the natural balance of coastal and island resources. The precise type of tourism desired and the strategy to be employed in fostering its growth must therefore be carefully considered and decided in advance, based on the environmental values and on alternative resource development.

57. The Management Plan should establish standards for resort

developments, covering (among others) the style and location of structures, treatment of sewage and control of litter, extent to which encroachment on the coastal zone is permitted, preservation of open spaces, and public use of and access to beaches. The Management Plan should also include the measures specified for overcoming the resource conflicts identified in Step 2.

58. **Step 6. Guide Construction Procedures.** Construction methods and materials should be designed to minimize impact on the environment.

59. As the scale of tourism increases, the supply of local materials may be overtaxed, requiring inappropriate exploitation of local resources. For example, living coral may be harvested to build roads at the cost of destroying fisheries breeding grounds and a major tourist attraction. Sand for construction may be dredged from in-shore waters, thereby causing turbidity and erosion which can have disastrous effects on lagoon or bay waters.

60. Natural beach erosion patterns should be understood before construction is begun; this is particularly true near high wave energy beaches. It is not unusual for land on beachfront property or near the end of a sedimentary island to erode at rates as high as several meters per year. In locations where this occurs the vulnerable zone should be zoned as an undeveloped buffer area and used for activities such as recreation which requires no permanent structures.

61. With development of tourism facilities, an increase in pollutants from within the tourist zone can be expected. The volume of solid wastes often mushrooms as personal incomes rise and more goods are imported from outside the zone. Adoption of outside consumer preferences further contribute to the process, rapidly overwhelming traditional methods of disposal. Sources of pollution from within the zone include:

- **Sewage.** The national parks authority should design procedures

to ensure that sewage is not directed to the beaches or swimming waters or the ground water which is used for the water supply; this will often require a major investment in a sewage system.

- **Pesticides**. The national parks authority should collaborate with the ministries of Agriculture and Health to design procedures to ensure that pesticides — used for example to control mosquitos or agricultural pests — do not drain into nearby rivers, swamps, lakes and coastal waters and affect protected areas, fisheries or swimming waters.

- **Refuse.** The national parks authority should design procedures to ensure that litter, garbage, trash, etc. is systematically collected. This will involve a preliminary inventory of solid waste generation, including long-term projections; investigation of public and private disposal practices; definition of criteria for disposal sites and their selection; and a strategy for charging the waste producer for costs of collection, handling and disposal. Disposal in the sea is to be avoided.

- **Noise.** Most tourist zones within national parks are based on aesthetic values which are greatly enhanced by tranquility. Few things are better calculated to destroy this asset than constant exposure to noise. If the area is attractive

The management plan for a park should establish standards for tourism development, covering the style, density and location of structures, in order to avoid overcrowded situations. Photo: Amboseli National Park, Kenya.

Photo by James W. Thorsell

primarily because of its peaceful setting, procedures should be designed to ensure that noise is kept unobtrusive. Examples include ensuring that airports are far removed from the area, discos are kept under control, loud motorcycles are discouraged, etc.

62. Aircraft noise is inherently extensive and can affect the entire Zone; its effect may be disproportionately greater in small national parks than in large parks so particular care needs to be given to finding alternatives to airports in small areas. Few national parks are sufficiently large that airports do not have an important negative impact.

63. **Step 7. Monitor Progress.** As planning is far from an exact science, every tourism development in a national park should have a built-in monitoring system for each of the major parameters: impact on the natural environment; resolution of conflicts over resources; implementation of Master Plan; regional cooperation; water supply and quality; impact and quality of construction activities; and control of pollution. For each of the parameters to be monitored, the national park authority should design a specific procedure and schedule for monitoring. Annual reports, for example, might be required for each.

IV.2 Zoning

64. Once boundaries in a protected area have been set, a system of evaluating and classifying land and water areas becomes necessary. This basic step of establishing management zones is taken to provide proper recognition and protection for park resources and greatly facilitates their proper management, including tourism aspects. As a tool for resource management, zones indicate where physical development can be located and, even more important, where it cannot be located. The zones proposed for each protected area must be consistent with the objectives for which the area was established, but in general a protected area can be divided into

zones of strict protection (some called a "sanctuary zone", where people are excluded), wilderness (where visitors are permitted only on foot), tourism (where visitors are encouraged in various compatible ways), and development (where facilities are concentrated). Tourism zones should contain representative samples of the park's important resources available for visitor appreciation. Such zones are sometimes divided into two types: extensive use, where park infrastructure, such as roads, trails, simple camp grounds and vista clearing, is permitted for low density recreational use; and intensive use, where relatively high concentrations of visitors are expected.

65. The latter type, usually comprising a small percentage of the park's area, will contain most of the park's visitor services, such as paved roads, visitor centres, visitor supply stores, formal camp grounds and overnight accommodations (if present). Because of the high density of use given to these zones, these are the lands most affected by visitor use and must therefore receive a high degree of management attention. The protected area authority should establish standards for tourism developments in the tourism zones such that the attractions of the protected area are enhanced. This will usually require that facilities placed in this zone are the minimum required to promote visitor enjoyment and safety, as well as resource protection.

66. When possible, hotels, restaurants, and stores should be located outside park boundaries so as to reduce human impact upon the protected area (FAO, 1988).

IV.3 Marketing

67. As in any other branch of tourism, nature tourism or ecotourism needs a sound and professional marketing approach if it is expected to succeed. For each protected area, it must be defined what marketing and publicity methods are to be used

(brochures, direct mail, TV, radio, newspapers, pamphlets, posters, etc.)

68.   Adequate information (together with visitation guidelines) on national parks and protected areas, including checklists of flora and fauna, must be placed in the hands of tour operators (both in-bound and foreign) for inclusion in their brochures and other materials for prospective visitors.

69.   A 12-bed photo safari camp in Africa may take only a few weeks to set up, but it may require two to three years to market it to the point where occupancy rates are generating an acceptable rate of return on capital.

70.   Even the name of a protected area should be marketable. The UNDP-WTO report on Uganda Tourism Development (1990) commenting on specific gorilla reserves, remarks that the native names of Mgahinga and Muhavura do not come easily to a foreign tourist; instead, the name "Uganda Gorilla Parks" would help ensure a more adequate market abroad. In the case of another reserve, the name Bwindi was deemed marketable, but it was suggested to be linked to the term Impenetrable Forest, a name which has proved to stir the imagination and may prompt people to visit Uganda simply as an exciting challenge.

IV.4   Parks and tourism in the regional context

71.   A major source of conflict between proponents of national parks and tourism is philosophical and ideological — resource protection versus development. Most of this conflict occurs not within the park boundaries but between the park and surrounding area. Adjacent community growth in response to tourist demand is often criticized as being incompatible with park values. Much of this conflict is based in the aesthetics of urbanized service centres.

72.   Another issue between national parks and tourism is that of jurisdiction. Although the national park is administered by one management

organization and set of policies, surrounding land is often under the control of many public and private sectors and stakeholders. Equally conflicting has been development by enterprises that lack adequate sensitivity to local conditions. Other conflicts arise between residents and tourism developers.

73.   Seldom are areas that include national parks planned as an integrated whole. Private enterprise is planned and developed on an individual site basis. The national park is also planned internally. These processes often result in: tourist congestion, erosion of resources, and a less-than satisfactory experience by visitors.

74.   All of the issues above can be solved but they require overall destination planning. The most logical beginning point for integrating the physical development of the park and its surrounding area is to review the present and potential markets (what travellers seek) and what the area has to offer (attractions, services, transportation).

For national parks, the travel market may be segmented along a scale from those seeking back-to-nature trekking to those satisfied with short, even vicarious, contact with a national park. Today, even though the former segment is growing, the great majority of travelers are satisfied with short-term contact and a well-interpreted description of the park features. Therefore, there is merit in

Whenever possible, hotels, restaurants, and other tourism facilities should be located outside park boundaries so as to reduce human impact upon the protected area, like the case of this motel near the entrance of Palenque National Park, Mexico, which has the added advantage of having incorporated traditional forms and materials (thatched roofs and local stone) into its architectural design. (IV. 2 Zoning)

Photo by Héctor Ceballos-Lascuráin

concentrating tourists where they can be managed.

75. Physical planning and design, when employing the talents and experience of professionals, can integrate community services, transportation and national park tourism. Commercial development, when properly designed, can be compatible with park values, reduce erosion and pollution of resources, and provide minimal impact.

76. Transportation and access for tourism need to be integrated with other purposes, such as industry and trade. Communities are usually the termini for air, land and water access. Physical planning for all travel modes, especially modern tour buses, needs to be integrated between outside and inside the park.

77. Often, a national park is but one attraction within a destination. Physical planning for tourism should reflect the visitors' interests and time periods for visiting several attractions within the destination, including a national park. Only by planning the overall destination can this be accomplished.

78. Worldwide, more and more architects, landscape architects and physical planning professionals are becoming experienced in tourism development. Destination areas can be attractively designed and made appropriate to all aesthetic values of a national park.

Design competitions and contractual agreements can tap the talent and experience of these professionals. In so doing, environmental resources can be protected, businesses can thrive, and social impacts can be minimized.

79. In a destination zone, including a national park, a great number of public and private stakeholders are involved. Needed are organizational mechanisms that foster an integration of leadership. For example, bureaucracies governing highways, airports, parks, and local infrastructure (water supply, waste disposal, police, fire protection) need the ability to cooperate with other tourism sectors (hotels, food services, attractions) when decisions on development plans and policies are made.

80. Communities and local areas need to prepare themselves for the potential threat of investors who see opportunities for development but lack sensitivity to local values. This preparedness may involve gaining financial support as well as establishing planning guidelines to protect valuable local resources as well as foster tourism development.

81. In many destinations that include national parks, the commercial enterprises that benefit from volumes of visitors to parks should provide the park with financial assistance. Because the parks attract visitors they are essential to the success of the tourist business sector.

*It is very important to review the existing facilities, an area has to offer regarding like this case in the Archeological Site of Chichén Itzá in Yucatán, Mexico, where an Historical **Hacienda** has been converted into a very attractive and comfortable hotel.*

Photo by Héctor Ceballos-Lascuráin

82. In order to avoid visitor confusion and disappointment, all promotional and informational activities for a destination should be coordinated. By planning these programs together, the private sector can avoid incorrect or overcapacity use of the national park.

Communities need to prepare themselves for the interest shown by outside investors who see opportunities for development but may lack sensitivity to appreciate local values, such as a typical village like this one in south-western Senegal.

Photo by Héctor Ceballos-Lascuráin

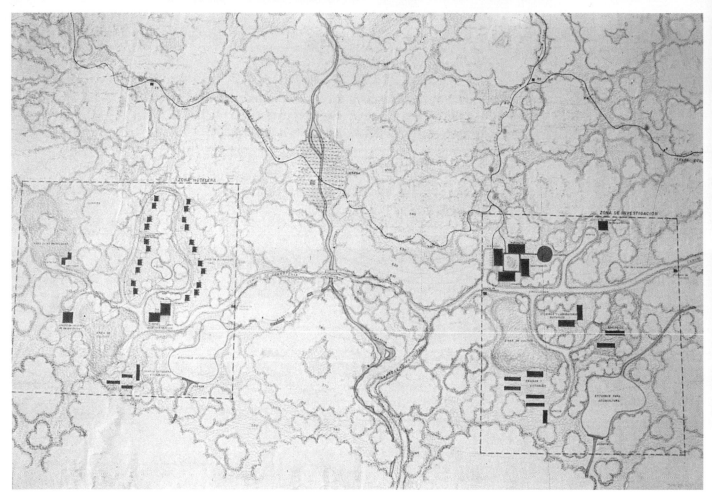

Specific site plans for infrastructure development should include careful zoning, adaptation to natural surroundings, and functional links between the tourism area and the park administration zone as shown in this preliminary design for an ecotourism centre in the Sian Ka'an Biosphere Reserve in Quintana Roo, Mexico.

Design and Photo by Héctor Ceballos-Lascuráin

*Two examples of wise adaptation of architectural design to natural features; a lodge in Aberdare National Park in Kenya makes good use of traditional building materials and an unobtrusive elevated structure that permits the free flow of wildlife underneath (**a**); the interpretive centre of Abuko Nature Reserve in Gambia includes this attractive observation area overlooking a marshy habitat (**b**).*

(a)

*Photos by James W Thorsell (**a**) and Héctor Ceballos-Lascuráin (**b**)*

(b)

CHAPTER V

GUIDELINES FOR DEVELOPMENT OF TOURIST FACILITIES IN NATIONAL PARKS

V.1 Site plans

83. In addition to the comprehensive management planning document there are specific site plans for infrastructure development. Detailed guidelines for development of tourist and park facilities are as follows:

- Man-made structures should interfere as little as possible with the natural ecosystem. Examples of bad siting include roads that block the flow of streams and thereby cause erosion on hillsides, structures which frighten wildlife from water sources, and effluent drains that pollute natural waterways.

- Structures must be as unobtrusive as possible. They should not dominate their natural surroundings nor detract from the intrinsic natural values of the area. They should be made of local materials whenever possible: stone, timber, bamboo, mud-brick, etc. Avoid alien materials such as asbestos sheeting, breeze blocks, etc. and garish colour schemes. Buildings should be in local styles and blend with their surroundings. If possible, buildings should be screened by natural bluffs or groves of trees.

If a tourist lodge is sited on a ridge with a commanding view over the whole area, the building will be visible from many aspects. However, if it is sited below the horizon and is single-storeyed and somber coloured, it will be far less obtrusive (Serena Lodge in Kenya's Masai Mara Reserve is an excellent example). Chan Chich Lodge in Belize is a good example of adequate use of local materials and architectural forms, and also a harmonious interrelation with the surrounding landscape.

- Suitable siting of buildings depends on functional considerations; it is not enough to consider only their strategic aspects. For example, guards will not inhabit posts unless they are serviced by reasonable access and water is available. These considerations may seem obvious but there are many examples where money has been wasted on uninhabited and uninhabitable guardposts, and on watchtowers located where there is nothing to watch.

- Before buildings are sited, some thought should be given to their accessibility and the flow of users. Tourist facilities should be separated from the administrative and workshop areas of a park headquarters if the two aspects are not to interfere with each other. It is better to service a group of buildings with a circular one-way flow road with a parking area set to one side than to have two-way traffic blocking the focal area of activity. Similarly, in an information centre, exhibits and panels should be arranged in a sequential order which draws visitors in a one-way flow around the room to the exit.

- The use of what is loosely termed as "ecotechniques" must be encouraged in the physical planning, architectural design and construction of tourism physical facilities (especially in isolated areas): solar energy (for heating water and, where appropriate, for generating electricity), capture and re-utilization of rainwater, recycling of garbage (organic and inorganic, solid and liquid), natural cross-ventilation instead of air-conditioning, a high level of self-sufficiency in food generation (through orchards, "ecological farms", aquaculture) etc.

- The architectural programme of ecotourism centres should include controlled access points and cabins, roads, self-guided nature trails, transportation options, interpretive centres, signs, observation towers and blinds, adequate but unpretentious lodging and dining facilities, docks (where needed), garbage disposal deposits, etc. Energy-saving criteria must be encouraged. Living quarters and facilities for park personnel and researchers should be included.

- Accommodations for nature tourists should be modest but comfortable, clean but unpretentious. This gives an added advantage to ecotourism over conventional or leisure tourism: the cost of an ecotourism centre is about four or five times lower per room unit (Ceballos- Lascuráin,

1986). The experience that an ecotourist seeks when he comes to a natural and exotic place is the opportunity of communion with nature and native cultures, of getting away from the concrete jungle and the luxuries and commodities of modern urban life.

- Roads and paths should be unobtrusive. Whenever possible, they should use the cover of dips in the land, trees, hills, and other features. They should flow with the land contours rather than cut across them. They should be designed to minimize erosion and therefore be of slight gradient with adequate drainage.

- Although roads may be built to bring visitors close to animals, they should avoid sensitive areas such as the breeding areas of waterbirds. They should employ bends or raised "humps" to control speed. Bends are also good for approaching wildlife and roads should be wide enough (or have special parking places) so that cars can pull off to view wildlife without obstructing other traffic.

84. In addition to these general guidelines, the following checklist provides design principles for evaluating the appropriateness and adequacy of specific site developments:

- *Everything must have a purpose* (relation of park to surroundings, relation of facility to use area and zones, relation of facilities in the site, relation to overall objectives of park master plan). Eliminate superfluous elements; where feasible, locate facilities on perimeters.

- *Design for people.* Recognize the optimal sociological use-limits of the site, as well as safety and convenience factors.

- *Design within the constraints of the resource.* Recognize the optimal environmental capacity of the site and potential impacts. Use the facility as a positive control in directing use; allow only day-use facilities in some areas.

- *Satisfy both form and function.* Balance economic, human, and resource values. Recognize design elements of exposure, dominance, texture, motif, form, and colour. Whenever possible use local building materials. Design with quality, utility and simplicity and build in local style. Landscape as appropriate to make buildings less obtrusive.

- *Provide facilities suited to the function* of the place, the *scale* of the place, and the *personalities* of the users.

- *Recognize technical requirements* (size, quantity, standards, orientation to weather and sun, convenience of access, utility costs).

- *Ensure efficient and safe operating use.* Where possible design for year-round use.

- *Investigate the long-term implications* of providing facilities, such as changing demands and technology, and continuing maintenance. Discourage undesirable uses.

- *If budgets are limited, start with simple but well-built camps* of bamboo, thatch, etc., which can be replaced with more permanent buildings later.

CHAPTER VI

SPORT HUNTING IN PROTECTED AREAS

85. National parks normally do not permit sport hunting, which can be a disastrous exposure of the protected populations to highly unnatural levels of disturbance and mortality, sometimes eliminating them from the reserve or at best rendering the hunted species very shy and difficult to see; hunting in such cases is usually inimical with nature-oriented tourism.

86. But sport hunting itself is a form of tourism, so other categories of protected areas, such as Game Reserves, often include hunting as a primary objective of management. Whether hunting should be allowed on land or buffer zones adjacent to a national park will depend very much on the individual situation; in some circumstances, a hunting reserve may be a useful extension of the protected habitat for the wildlife and a useful source of local employment, revenue, meat, and other useful products. Controlled hunting by either locals or sportsmen may also be useful in eliminating animals which leave reserves to raid neighbouring agricultural crops for food or as compensation for the damage such animals cause.

87. In some national parks, hunting is allowed as a means to reduce numbers of alien species. Examples include the hunting of feral pigs and goats in Hawaii Volcanoes National Park and deer and elk in some New Zealand national parks. In any case, sport hunting is an exceptional case not normally addressed as a management issue relating to national parks and it is only briefly treated here.

88. The successful and profitable running of a hunting reserve is highly technical and outside the scope of this paper (useful references include: Leopold, 1933; Caughley, 1977; Van Lavieren, 1983). In summary, such reserves must have satisfactory measures for:

- determining the methods of hunting;

- delimiting the area in which hunting is permitted;

- controlling the number of licensed hunters using the area;

- limiting the hunting period;

- setting balanced quotas and bag limits;

- optimising off-take;

- controlling the quota of harvestable animals;

- controlling the age/sex classes of animals hunted: e.g. hunting of females may be prohibited;

- monitoring off-take for numbers, quality and hunter effort;

- controlling the types of firearms and ammunition used;

- having trained staff to dispatch injured animals;
- instituting safeguards to prevent accidents to hunters or staff;
- protecting protected species in the hunting area;
- providing facilities for the cleaning of trophies and for the storage and utilization of carcasses;
- collecting revenues (licence fees and kill or bag taxes).

LEARNING ABOUT PROTECTED AREAS

The most direct way for the general public to learn about a protected area is to see it themselves. The basic gear required by an ecotourist is shown here: binoculars, photo equipment, local field guides, brochures, maps, species checklists, and a hat. (VII. 1)

Photo by Héctor Ceballos-Lascuráin

CHAPTER VII

GUIDELINES FOR PROVIDING EDUCATION AND INTERPRETATION PROGRAMMES

VII.1 The role of education and interpretation

89. Education and interpretation are seen as key tools used by managers to better manage tourists. In fact, it has been said that not having an interpretation programme in a park is like inviting a visitor to your house, opening the door and then disappearing!

90. The most direct way for the general public to learn about the protected area is to see it themselves. It is crucial that they get a good first impression. It must always be remembered that educating the public is not an end in itself for the protected area, but a means to an end. The reserve needs the support and goodwill of its visitors. They must be made to feel welcome. The way in which the manager addresses the public is through Information and Interpretation Services.

91. Interpretation services in national parks differs from information provision in that it is not merely a listing of facts but tries to reveal concepts, meanings and the interrelationships of natural phenomena. Interpretation serves to awaken public awareness of

park purposes and policies and strives to develop a concern for protection. It should also educate the visitor to appreciate what the protected area means to the region and the nation. Interpretation should fill the visitor with a greater sense of wonder and curiosity about the natural surroundings and make his (or her) visit to the area more rewarding.

92. It is the opportunity of "first-hand experience" with the "real thing" that provides the principal distinction between interpretation and education. For example, an interpretative centre in a national park will introduce, clarify, and direct the visitor to the actual resource outside, whereas a museum building in a city generally functions as a destination in itself. A publication titled, "The Birds of Manu National Park — and Where to Find Them" would clearly be interpretative; whereas, "The Population Dynamics and Reproduction of Umbrella Birds", in itself, would not.

93. The objective of the visitor interpretation service should be to provide information, entertainment, stimulation and education in a pleasant and fascinating setting in order to win

visitor support for the type of management being applied. It is thus a management tool, influencing behaviour, soliciting support and making the manager's job easier (see Sharpe, 1976).

94. Most of the visitor information and interpretation service will be presented within the protected area, and the local villages in the reserve's immediate surroundings. It is also important to advertise outside the reserve to attract visitors in the first place. They must know about the reserve, where it is, and what they can do there. The information service covers everything from brochures to film shows but the following types of information will generally need to be included in the protected area information service:

- **What there is to see and do** — visitors will need this information to plan their visit and make best use of their time in relation to their particular interests. This information must also include the seasonal or daily options (e.g., there is a collection of scavengers around a carcass today).

- **How to see what you want — maps of the reserve** and points of interest, with information on how to get there, distances, time, hardships involved, and hazards.

- **What visitors are looking at** — basic information should be presented simply and briefly, but in an interesting fashion so that the visitor gains a greater understanding of what he experiences. This is where simple information is translated into interpretation.

- **How to behave in the reserve** — as well as explaining the regulations of what is and is not allowed in the reserve, information should also be given on how to behave so as not to disturb current management operations, other visitors, and the natural features. Visitors should be cautioned not to misuse the reserve facilities, nor to deface physical

features. Visitors should be acquainted with the basic etiquette of reserve use — no radios, no vandalism or graffiti, no littering, no collection of fauna or plant materials, no disturbance of wildlife (feeding, chasing, or tampering with nests), keep to designated trails or camp areas, and obey any relevant safety warnings. Visitors should be made aware of the maxim "take nothing but photos, leave nothing but footprints".

- **Why have a reserve at all** — answer the basic questions. What is the purpose of protected areas? And why here? Explain the relationship of the protected area to its surrounding lands and in importance in the world system of protected areas.

- **What is there to attract visitors to come back again** — give suggestions for trips of differing durations, centred on different locations, trips with different themes, e.g. wildlife viewing, birdwatching, hiking, camping. Mention noteworthy seasonal happenings, e.g. arrival of migratory birds or calving periods.

A good sign like this one in Shannon National Park, Australia, can provide excellent orientation regarding adequate behaviour in a protected area.

Photo by Héctor Ceballos-Lascuráin

- **How visitors can help** — suggest ways in which impressed or interested visitors can help by becoming supporters of the reserve or of conservation organizations. Provide addresses of local clubs, societies, volunteer organizations, local political leaders and wildlife magazines.

VII.2 Techniques

95. There are numerous techniques available to communicate information about the protected area, some of them very simple. All have their particular uses and it is wise to use several methods to get maximum effect. People differ very much in their needs and expectations and it is important to cater for different tastes. The dedicated and experienced animal watcher, for instance, will be happy to put up with considerable hardships and find out information for himself.

The challenge to the manager is to attract not just the specialists but a wider audience from among the general public and to stimulate and enhance their appreciation of the area.

96. Some people prefer to be organized in groups and presented with a standard explanation by a guide, others prefer to find their own way around a trail system with the aid of an explanatory and informative brochure; yet others resent any attempt at

organization and want to "go it alone". Some people like to talk, some to listen, some to read information, others to see things. Below is a list of the most widely used methods for communicating with visitors and some hints as to their use.

97. **Brochures and leaflets.** These should be as colourful, attractive and interesting as possible. Leaflets should tantalize rather than fulfil. They are for wide distribution in tourist offices and the like. They should lure visitors to the reserve, give information on what can be seen and done there, how to get there and any special preparations required (e.g., bookings, permits, special equipment, clothes or food). The leaflet should outline the conditions and facilities available in and around the reserve and current costs of accommodation, or other expenditures. Brochures (available in several different languages if possible) provide the visitor inside the reserve with basic information to help him or her enjoy and make the most of his or her visit. This usually includes brief descriptions of the main attractions, a map, and a list of the park regulations. It is useful if the folded brochure fits comfortably into a pocket; then it is more likely to be kept. An excellent example is the brochure for Peru's Manu National Park.

98. **Specialized guides, keys and checklists.** These are often appreciated by visitors with particular interests or those unfamiliar with the area, and sales of such items from park offices may help cover some of the park running costs.

99. **Self-guided trails.** These are trails of varying lengths, though usually fairly short, where groups or individual visitors stop to view features of interest. Visitors are provided with brochures which give them information about individual sites which are marked in some way, perhaps by a numbered post. Alternatively, the information may be on sign boards along the trail but these are less desirable as they tend to impinge on the natural surroundings and require greater maintenance, unless made of weather-resistant material such as stainless steel. In addition, a brochure

Guides, brochures and checklists are appreciated by visitors, as seen here at the publications display area of the information centre in Glacier National Park, Montana, USA.

Photo by James W. Thorsell

can be taken home, shown to other people and thus multiply the education impact of the self-guided trail.

100. Here, a guide accompanies parties of visitors around a system of routes by foot, horse, boat, bus, or other means, pointing out and discussing natural features along the way. Such a tour has the advantage that the guide can adapt what he says to the particular group of visitors but this obviously requires more manpower than a system of self-guided trails. The method is especially useful with school children and tour groups when the guide may be the schoolteacher or tour leader and not one of the reserve staff. In any case guides must be fluent in the languages of park visitors.

101. **Wilderness trails.** These are simply well-marked trails for visitors to explore on their own on a "see and discover" basis. Primitive camping sites and shelters may be provided.

102. **Visitor information centres.** These are special buildings in which more detailed information about the reserve can be displayed. Exhibits may include photographs arranged in wall or panel displays, map models of the reserve, mounted specimens or animal remains, diagrams of food chains, etc. Visitor centres are very useful for providing interest for visitors trapped by bad weather, or while they are waiting (e.g., for a tour guide or while a permit is being checked) or who want more information about the park. They are useful for showing natural processes, life histories and other features of the park that cannot be seen on a short visit, and what happens in the park at night or in other seasons. Where necessary, information centres can be enlarged or combined with education centres. Good examples are found in Royal Chitwan National Park in Nepal, Shannon National Park in Australia and Abuko Nature Reserve in Gambia.

103. **Education centres.** These are special buildings capable of mounting more formal educational displays. They usually have facilities to hold classes or discussion sessions and are often

equipped with audio-visual equipment for slideshows or films. Permanent ongoing audiovisual presentations may be exhibited in education centres or information centres. Good examples are found in Murchison Falls National Park, Uganda, and Volcan Poas National Park in Costa Rica.

104. **Botanic gardens or animal orphanages**. These are interesting sites where visitors can get a closer view of some of the plants or animals found in the reserve and identify better some of the things they have seen in the wild. They sometimes combine with other functions such as a reserve orphanage, hospital or rehabilitation centre where young or sick animals are being nursed or trained to be eventually returned to the wild. For instance, orangutan rehabilitation stations in reserves in Sumatra and East Malaysia that attract many visitors and information centres at such sites can be used to disseminate information about the whole reserve. Botanical plots can also serve as research plots as in the Cibodas Botanic Gardens in Indonesia and botanic gardens on many of the islands of the West Indies.

105. **Informal contact.** Park staff moving about their normal duties will casually engage visitors in conversation as they meet them, asking how they are enjoying themselves, what they like to see, and giving relevant current information, e.g., where animals have been recently sighted, lion kills and so

A good, knowledgeable guide who communicates valuable information on a protected area, as shown here aboard a tour boat in the Galápagos National Parks, is indispensable in a guided ecotour.

Photo by Héctor Ceballos-Lascuráin

*Adequate visitor information centres, as these two examples from Shannon National Park in Australia (**a**) and Abuko Nature Reserve in Gambia (**b**), play vital roles in the interpretation of a protected area.*

Photos by Héctor Ceballos-Lascuráin

(a)

(b)

Informal contact between park staff and visitors, as shown here in Westlands World Heritage Site, New Zealand, is normally mutually beneficial.

Photo by James W. Thorsell

on. All park staff must, therefore, be fairly proficient in recognizing wildlife and knowledgeable about the natural history of the park, and may require some training in visitor communication.

106. **Visitor opinion, gathering feedback.** Communication is a two-way process. The park manager wants to know whether he is getting his message across and what the visiting public think about the park, what queries they have (this will shape the content of information services) and whether they have comments, advice, requests or complaints. Feedback comes from direct discussion, invited comments in visitor books and suggestion boxes.

107. A number of good reference manuals give further details on developing information and interpretative

facilities in protected areas, (e.g., Sharpe, 1976; Berkmuller, 1981); Ashbaugh, 1973; Manly, 1977; Christiansen, 1977).

VII.3 Exhibit planning guidelines

108. Displays and exhibits have advantages as communications media in a protected area:

- they are continuously available;

- they are "self-pacing";

- they can use original objects and specimens;

- they can be located indoors or outdoors, and can be portable.

109. **Exhibit planning guidelines.** The following guidelines may assist in preparing attractive exhibits:

- choose a theme, e.g. tropical rainforest;

- identify the audience and aim to meet its needs;

- define the objectives, e.g. education, entertainment, motivation, or public relations;

- decide what type(s) to build, e.g. panels (text, diagrams, photographs), objects and specimens, dioramas, scale models, live exhibits.

110. **Factors in exhibit design.** Factors to consider when designing exhibits for tourists, including local, national, and international, include:

- location (inside, outside, in visitor centre);

- mobility and portability for use in schools, fairs;

- durability (and resistance to vandalism);

- position (preferably eye level) and viewing distance;

- lighting and sunlight's effects on colours;

- availability of materials, e.g. glass;

- attention-getting title;

- brief, readable, provocative labels;

- effectiveness of specimens and adequacy of accompanying text;

- exhibit sequence, use of partitions;

- maintenance and deterioration (if you can't maintain it, don't build it!);

- use of pesticides and fungicides;

- desirability of visitor participation exhibits, e.g. wheel display, guessing games, peep box, electric panels;

- live animal exhibits, e.g. terrariums, aquariums;

- plant, rock, and insect collections (must be attractively presented and interpretive);

- animal exhibits (obtained from road kills, mounted study skins, bird feeders, plaster casts or tracks, spoor).

VII.4 Guidelines for developing nature trails in protected areas

111. One of the best ways to encourage visitors to experience the park is through developing interesting walks which will bring them into controlled contact with the major attractions of the park. The following points should be borne in mind when developing nature trails (Ashbaugh and Kordish, 1971; Sharpe, 1976; Berkmuller, 1981; Thorsell, 1984):

A. General characteristics:

- A nature trail should be **short** (0.5 to 1.5 km), with a walking time of 30 to 60 minutes.

- Ideally, a nature trail is constructed as a **one-way loop** beginning and ending in the same place.

- A nature trail is **information**. Along the trail are signs or labels explaining its features. Signs can contain all the desired information, or simply have numbers referring the visitor to an accompanying pamphlet.

- A nature trail is **inviting**. It must have a clear, well marked beginning. It should be wide and flat enough to walk in comfort. It should have no steep climbs, muddy places, or physical obstacles.

- A nature trail is clean and **well maintained**. Litter cans are often provided at the entrance and at rest

Signs along nature trails should communicate valuable information to visitors, as shown by these two examples from Yellowstone National Park, US, (a) and (b).

Photos by Héctor Ceballos Lascuráin

(a)

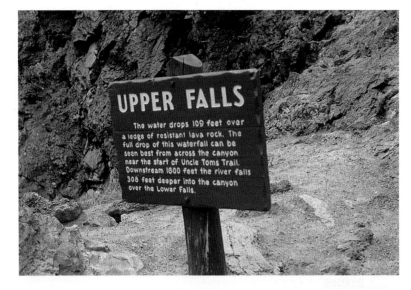

(b)

stops. Vegetation and debris are regularly removed from the trail.

B. Developing and constructing a trail:

- Conduct a thorough survey of the area where the trail is to pass. Make a list of all notable natural and historic features (e.g. salt licks, rock outcrops, viewpoints, vegetation, fossils, waterfalls). Mark these features on a sketch map and arrange a trail route to connect them.

- Walk the route to check its length and access to noted features and to determine the feasibility of trail construction.

- Disturb the natural scene as little as possible. Avoid unnecessary damage during construction by supervising workers carefully.

- Clear the walking area of all obstacles along the trail and cut overhanging vegetation to a height of 2m. Avoid cutting large trees, and do not clear all debris down to bare soil. Fill depressions with rock or earth waste.

- Build the trail with curves, avoiding straight stretches where possible. A winding trail is more interesting to walk. Avoid designs that "double back", which may encourage visitors to take short cuts.

- Avoid steep hillsides and waterlogged areas. Ensure that drainage runs off, not down, the trail; install water bars and drains. In some areas the trail may need to be raised on a wooden walkway or stepping stones.

- At rest stops provide simple benches. At stream crossings or deep gorges it may be necessary to build bridges. Steps may be cut in rock, or a fallen tree may be used for passage if it is wide enough for safety.

- Provide a trail entrance sign with basic information (a map and the trail's length). Directional signs may be required at junctions.

C. Interpreting the landscape along the trail:

- If possible, determine a theme (e.g., "Vegetation of the Picachos Mountains") for the trail, and give the trail a name (e.g., "Mountain Forest Nature Trail") reflecting that theme. This adds to the interest and appeal of the trail.

- Decide between (a) printed labels along the trail and (b) numbered labels referring to a printed leaflet.

- At least 12 features, and at most 30, should be identified for interpretation. Information should be accurate, interesting, brief, and easy to understand.

- A map must be provided, either on a sign or in a leaflet. Also consider providing a checklist of "things to see along the trail". A leaflet, if used, need not be expensive but should include sketches and diagrams and be visually attractive.

VII.5 Suggested approaches to interpretation in marine parks

112. Marine parks have a number of differences from terrestrial parks which require somewhat different approaches to interpretation. Marine interpretation programmes may take the form of guided or self-guided trails. Examples are: boardwalks through coastal wetlands, underwater trails, such as through the reefs at Buck Island National Monument in the US Virgin Islands, or underwater viewing chambers such as are found at Green Island on the Great Barrier Reef (Australia) and several marine parks in Japan. Off-site interpretive programmes involve publications, lectures and film or slide shows given either on the site, or at schools, community centres and other institutions, or through broadcast television.

VII.6 Park staff behaviour

113. Since support for the park system ultimately depends on public goodwill, staff should be helpful, courteous and polite at all times even if the visitors are sometimes a nuisance. Protected area staff must always set a good example to visitors and must themselves observe park regulations at all times. Staff should pick up litter even if they are accompanying visitors, and put it in the proper receptacles. Park staff should not feed nor frighten wildlife and should discourage visitors (or tour leaders) from doing so.

114. Where necessary, staff must be prepared to be firm but courteous with those dropping litter, graffiti artists, and people making too much noise or disturbing wildlife or other visitors. They may have to put out fires made in the wrong places, order removal of tents to proper campsites, or recall visitors from prohibited areas. Sometimes it may be necessary to enforce limits on how many visitors can enter a park or part of a park. It may even be necessary to periodically close a park to visitors in "unsafe" times (e.g., floods, avalanches, fog, drought), critical wildlife breeding seasons or periods of adverse weather, or to give the staff a chance to repair damaged facilities and clean the area up for another visitor influx.

115. By observing public behaviour on a protected area, management personnel will usually find there is need for additional interpretive effort. For example, although collection of living molluscs may be prohibited, shells occupied by hermit crabs are often collected, the people not realizing that crabs too are protected animal life. Special efforts should be made by the area manager and staff to observe the actions of visitors, particularly on days of high visitor use and in unattended campground and picnic areas and heavily used undeveloped areas.

VII.7 Tourist Code of Ethics

116. The national park manager should work with the national tourism

promotion agency to prepare and widely distribute a code of conduct for all tourists to the country. This should be available in the appropriate language versions and be promoted as well by all private tour operators. An example from Nepal is attached in Annex I. This Code should be in general agreement with WTO's "Tourism Bill of Rights and Tourist Code".

ANNEX I

THE KATHMANDU DECLARATION ON MOUNTAIN ACTIVITIES

Preamble

The International Union of Alpine Associations (IUAA) met in Kathmandu from the 10th to 16th October 1982, for the 44th General Assembly and celebrated the 50th anniversary of its founding.

It was for the first time in the history of the IUAA that such an important meeting was held in Asia - most appropriately in the lap of the mighty Himalayas.

One hundred and thirty-five delegates from twenty-six countries exchanged ideas and experiences on various problems related with mountaineering activities.

On evaluating the problems pertaining to the mountains, a new consensus has emerged in the conference. The IUAA General Assembly has resolved to adopt the following principles and guidelines as a programme for concrete action to be henceforth called the Kathmandu Declaration on Mountain Activities:

Articles of the Declaration

1.   There is an urgent need for effective protection of the mountain environment and landscape.

2.   The flora, fauna and natural resources of all kinds need immediate attention care and concern.

3.   Actions designed to reduce the negative impact of man's activities on mountains should be encouraged.

4.   The cultural heritage and the dignity of the local population are inviolable.

5.   All activities designed to restore and rehabilitate the mountain world need to be encouraged.

6.   Contacts between mountaineers of different regions and countries should be increasingly encouraged in the spirit of friendship, mutual respect and peace.

7.   Information and education for improving the relationship between man and his environment should be available for wider and wider sections of society.

8.   The use of appropriate technology for energy needs and the proper disposal of waste in the mountain areas are matters of immediate concern.

9.   The need for more international support - governmental as well as non-governmental - to the developing mountain countries, for instance, in matters of ecological conservation.

10.   The need for widening access to mountain areas in order to promote their appreciation and study should be unfettered by political considerations.

ANNEX II

TOURISM BILL OF RIGHTS AND TOURIST CODE

The General Assembly of the World Tourism Organization at its sixth ordinary session held at Sofia (People's Republic of Bulgaria) from 17 to 26 September 1985:

1.   AWARE of the importance of tourism in the life of peoples because of its direct and positive effects on the social, economic, cultural and educational sectors of national society and the contribution it can make, in the spirit of the United Nations Charter and the Manila Declaration on World Tourism, to improving mutual understanding, bringing peoples closer together and, consequently, strengthening international cooperation,

2.   RECALLING that, as recognized by the General Assembly of the United Nations, the World Tourism Organization has a central and decisive role in the development of tourism with a view to contributing, in accordance with Article 3, paragraph 1 of its Statutes, "to economic development, international understanding, peace, prosperity and universal respect for, and observation of, human rights and fundamental freedoms for all without distinction as to race, sex, language or religion",

3.   RECALLING the Universal Declaration of Human Rights adopted by the General Assembly of the United Nations on 10 December 1948, and in particular Article 24 which provides that "Everyone has the right to rest and leisure, including reasonable limitation of working hours and periodic holidays with pay", as well as the International Covenant on Economic, Social and Cultural rights adopted by the General Assembly of the United Nations on 16 December 1966, which invites States to ensure for everyone "Rest, leisure and reasonable limitation of working hours and periodic holidays with pay, as well as remuneration for public holidays",

4.   CONSIDERING the resolution and recommendations adopted by the United Nations Conference on International Travel and Tourism (Rome, September 1963), and particularly those aimed at promoting tourism development in the various countries and at simplifying government formalities in respect of international travel,

5.   DRAWING ITS INSPIRATION from the principles set forth in the Manila Declaration on World Tourism adopted by the World Tourism Conference on 10 October 1980, which emphasizes the true, human dimension of tourism, recognizes the new role of tourism as an appropriate instrument for

improving the quality of life of all peoples and as a vital force for peace and international understanding and defines the responsibility of States for developing tourism and, in particular, for fostering awareness of tourism among the peoples of the world and protecting and enhancing the tourism resources which are part of mankind's heritage, with a view to contributing to the establishment of a new international economic order,

6.　SOLEMNLY AFFIRMING, as a natural consequence of the right to work, the fundamental right of everyone, as already sanctioned by the Universal Declaration of Human Rights, to rest, leisure and periodic holidays with pay and to use them for holiday purposes, to travel freely for education and pleasure and to enjoy the advantages of tourism, both within his country of residence and abroad,

7.　INVITES the States to draw inspiration from the principles set forth below constituting the Tourism Bill of Rights and Tourist Code, and to apply them in accordance with the procedures prescribed in the legislation and regulations of their own countries.

TOURISM BILL OF RIGHTS

Article I

1.　The right of everyone to rest and leisure, reasonable limitation of working hours, periodic leave with pay and freedom of movement without limitation, within the bounds of the law, is universally recognized.

2.　The exercise of this right constitutes a factor of social balance and enhancement of national and universal awareness.

Article II

As a consequence of this right, the States should formulate and implement policies aimed at promoting the harmonious development of domestic and international tourism and leisure activities for the benefit of all those taking part in them.

Article III

To this end the States should:

(a) encourage the orderly and harmonious growth of both domestic and international tourism;

(b) integrate their tourism policies with their overall development policies at all levels - local, regional, national and international - and broaden tourism cooperation within both a bilateral and multilateral framework, including that of the World Tourism Organization;

(c) give due attention to the principles of the Manila Declaration on World Tourism and the Acapulco Document "while formulating and implementing, as appropriate, their tourism policies, plans and programmes, in accordance with their national priorities and within the framework of the programme of work of the World Tourism Organization";*

(d) encourage the adoption of measures enabling everyone to participate in domestic and international tourism, especially by a better allocation of work and leisure time, the establishment or improvement of systems of annual leave with pay and the staggering of holiday dates and by particular attention to tourism for the young, elderly and disabled; and

(e) in the interest of present and future generations, protect the tourism environment which, being at once human, natural, social and cultural, is the legacy of all mankind.

* Resolution 38/146 adopted by the United Nations General Assembly at its thirty-eighth session on 19 December 1983.

Article IV

The States should also:

(a) encourage the access of domestic and international tourists to the heritage of the host communities by applying the provisions of existing facilitation instruments issuing from the United Nations, the International Civil Aviation Organization, the International Maritime Organization, the Customs Co-operation Council or from any other body, the World Tourism Organization in particular, with a view to increasingly liberalizing travel;

(b) promote tourism awareness and facilitate contact between visitors and host communities with a view to their mutual understanding and betterment;

(c) ensure the safety of visitors and the security of their belongings through preventive and protective measures;

(d) afford the best possible conditions of hygiene and access to health services as well as of the prevention of communicable diseases and accidents;

(e) prevent any possibility of using tourism to exploit others for prostitution purposes; and

(f) reinforce, for the protection of tourists and the population of the host community, measures to prevent the illegal use of narcotics.

Article V

The States should lastly:

(a) permit domestic and international tourists to move freely about the country, without prejudice to any limitative measures taken in the national interest concerning certain areas of the territory;

(b) not allow any discriminatory measures in regard to tourists;

(c) allow tourists prompt access to administrative and legal services and to consular representatives, and make available internal and external public communications; and

(d) contribute to the information of tourists with a view to fostering understanding of the customs of the populations constituting the host communities at places of transit and sojourn.

Article VI

1. The populations constituting the host communities in places of transit and sojourn are entitled to free access to their own tourism resources while fostering respect, through their attitude and behaviour, for their natural and cultural environment.

2. They are also entitled to expect from tourists understanding of and respect for their customs, religions and other elements of their cultures which are part of the human heritage.

3. To facilitate such understanding and respect, the dissemination of appropriate information should be encouraged on:

(a) the customs of host communities, their traditional and religious practices, local taboos and sacred sites and shrines which must be respected;

(b) their artistic, archaeological and cultural treasures which must be preserved; and

(c) wildlife and other natural resources which must be protected.

Article VII

The populations constituting the host communities in places of transit and sojourn are invited to receive tourists with the greatest possible hospitality, courtesy and respect necessary for the development of harmonious human and social relations.

Article VIII

1.   Tourism professionals and suppliers of tourism and travel services can make a positive contribution to tourism development and to implementation of the provisions of this Bill of Rights.

2.   They should conform to the principles of this Bill of Rights and honour commitments of any kind entered into within the context of their professional activities, ensuring the provision of quality products so as to help affirm the humanist nature of tourism.

3.   They should in particular refrain from encouraging the use of tourism for all forms of exploitation of others.

Article IX

Encouragement should be given to tourism professionals and suppliers of tourism and travel services by granting them, through appropriate national and international legislation, the necessary facilities to enable them to:

(a) exercise their activities in favourable conditions, free from any particular impediment or discrimination;

(b) benefit from general and technical training schemes, both within their countries and abroad, so as to ensure the availability of skilled manpower; and

(c) cooperate among themselves as well as with the public authorities, through national and international organizations, with a view to improving the coordination of their activities and the quality of their services.

TOURIST CODE

Article X

Tourists should, by their behaviour, foster understanding and friendly relations among peoples, at both the national and international levels, and thus contribute to lasting peace.

Article XI

1.   At places of transit and sojourn tourists must respect the established political, social, moral and religious order and comply with the legislation and regulations in force.

2.   In these places tourists must also:

(a) show the greatest understanding for the customs, beliefs and behaviour of the host communities and the greatest respect for their natural and cultural heritage;

(b) refrain from accentuating the economic, social and cultural differences between themselves and the local population;

(c) be receptive to the culture of the host communities, which is an integral part of the common human heritage;

(d) refrain from exploiting others for prostitution purposes; and

(e) refrain from trafficking in, carrying or using narcotics and/or other prohibited drugs.

Article XII

During their travel from one country to another and within the host country tourists should be able, by appropriate government measures, to benefit from:

(a) relaxation of administrative and financial controls; and

(b) the best possible conditions of transport and sojourn that can be offered by suppliers of tourism services.

Article XIII

1.   Tourists should be afforded free access, both within and outside their countries, to sites and places of tourist interest and, subject to existing regulations and limitations, freedom of movement in places of transit and sojourn.

2.   On access to sites and places of tourist interest and throughout their transit and sojourn, tourists should be able to benefit from:

(a) objective, precise and complete information on conditions and facilities provided during their travel and sojourn by official tourism bodies and suppliers of tourism services;

(b) safety of their persons, security of their belongings and protection of their rights as consumers;

(c) satisfactory public hygiene, particularly so far as accommodation, catering and transport are concerned, information on the effective prevention of communicable diseases and accidents and ready access to health services;

(d) access to swift and efficient public communications, both internal and external;

(e) administrative and legal procedures and guarantees necessary for the protection of their rights; and

(f) the practice of their own religion and the use of existing facilities for that purpose.

Article XIV

Everyone is entitled to make his needs known to legislative representatives and public authorities so that he may exercise his right to rest and leisure in order to enjoy the benefits of tourism under the most favourable conditions and, where appropriate and to the extent consistent with law, associate with others for that purpose.

REFERENCES

Alcances, Ray P., Amelia Supetran, and M.B. Anderson. 1983. **Environmental Impact Assessment Handbook**. Ministry of Human Settlements, Manila. 242 pp.

Ashbaugh, Byron L. 1973. **Planning a Nature Center**. National Audubon Society. New York. 88 pp.

Ashbaugh, B.L. and R.J. Kordis. 1971. **Trail Planning and Layout**. National Audubon Society. New York. 75 pp.

Baker, Priscilla R. 1990. **Tourism and Protection of Natural Areas**. National Park Service. Washington, D.C. 21 pp.

Berkemuller, Klaus. 1981. **Education about the Tropical Rain Forest**. IUCN, Gland. Switzerland (also available in Spanish and French).

Bosselman, Fred P. 1978. **In the Wake of the Tourist**. The Conservation Foundation, Washington D.C. 278 pp.

Boullón, Roberto C. 1985. **Planificación del Espacio Turístico**. Editorial Trillas, Mexico. 245 pp.

Budowski, Gerardo. 1977. Tourism and Conservation: Conflict, Coexistence or Symbiosis? **Parks** 1(4). 4 pp.

Ceballos-Lascuráin, Héctor. 1986. **Estudio de Prefactibilidad Socioeconómica del Turismo Ecológico y Anteproyecto Arquitectónico y Urbanístico del Centro de Turismo Ecológico de Sian Ka'an, Quintana Roo**. Study made for SEDUE, México.

Ceballos-Lascuráin, Héctor. 1988. **The Future of Ecotourism**, in Mexico Journal, January 17: pp. 13-14.

Ceballos-Lascuráin, Héctor. 1990. **Tourism, Ecotourism and Protected Areas**. Paper presented at the CNPPA 34th Working Session, Perth, Australia.

Christiansen, Monty L. 1977. **Park Planning Handbook, Fundamentals of Physical Planning for Parks and Recreation Areas**. John Wiley and Sons. New York. 413 pp.

Dasmann, Raymond F., John P. Milton and Peter H. Freeman. 1973. **Ecological Principles for Economic Development**. John Wiley and Sons Ltd. Letchworth, U.K. 252 pp.

Eidsvik, Harold K. 1980. **Tourism in Relation to Protected Areas**. Unpublished. CNPPA paper. 5 pp.

English, P. 1986. **The Great Escape? An Examination of North-South Tourism**. North-South Institute, Ottawa. 89 pp.

FAO. 1988. **National Parks Planning: A Manual with Annotated Examples**. Food and Agriculture Organization of the United Nations. Rome. 33 pp.

Geoghegan, Tighe, Ivor Jackson, Allen Putney and Yves Renard. 1984. **Environmental Guidelines for Development in the Lesser Antilles**. Caribbean Conservation Association, St. Croix.

International Union of Official Travel Organizations. 1973. **National Parks and Wildlife Areas as Tourist**

Resources. World Tourism Organization. Madrid, Spain. 37 pp.

IUCN. 1990. **1990 UN List of National Parks and Protected Areas**. IUCN/WCMC. Gland, Switzerland/Cambridge, UK. 275 pp.

Lawson, Fred and Manuel Baud-Bovy. 1977. **Tourism and Recreation Development**. CBI Publishing Company Inc. Massachusetts, USA. 210 pp.

Lindberg, Kreg. 1991. **Policies for Maximizing Nature Tourism's Ecological and Economic Benefits**. World Resources Institute. Washington, D.C. 37 pp.

Manly, R.J. (ed.) 1977. **Guidelines for Interpretative Building Design**. National Audubon Society. New York City. 52 pp.

MacKinnon, John and K., Graham Child and Jim Thorsell. 1987. **Managing Protected Areas in the Tropics**. IUCN, 1987. 295 pp.

McEachern, John and Edward L. Towle. 1974. **Ecological guidelines for island development**. IUCN Publication (N.S.) 30: 1-66.

Odum, William E. 1976. **Ecological guidelines for tropical coastal development**. IUCN (N.S.) 42: 1-61.

Salm, Rod and John Clark. 1984. **Marine and Coastal Protected Areas: A guide for planners and managers**. IUCN, Gland, Switzerland. 302 pp.

Sharpe, Grant. 1976. **Interpreting our Environment**. Wiley. New York City.

Singh, Tej Vir, Jagdish Kaur and D.P. Singh. 1982. **Studies in Tourism, Wildlife, Parks, Conservation**. Metropolitan Books Co. Ltd. New Delhi, India. 300 pp.

South Magazine. August 1989. **Riding the Tourist Boom**. pp. 12.

Thorsell, J.W. 1984. **Protected Areas in East Africa: A Training Manual**. College of African Wildlife Management, Tanzania.

UNDP-WTO. 1990 (in press). **Uganda Tourism Development Projects Report**. UNDP-WTO. (Restricted).

UNEP-WTO. 1983. **Workshop on Environmental Aspects of Tourism**. UNEP-WTO. 114 pp.

UNEP 1984. Industry and Environment review No. 1. Vol. 7. "**Tourism and the Environment**".

UNEP 1986. Industry and Environment review No. 1. Vol. 9. "**Carrying Capacity for Tourism Activities**".

University of the South Pacific. 1980. **Pacific Tourism - As Islands See It**. Fiji. 171 pp.

Western D. 1982. Human Values and the Conservation of a Savanna Ecosystem. **In**: McNeely and Miller (eds.) **National Parks, Conservation and Development**, Smithsonian Press.

Western D. and W.R. Henry. 1979. **Economics and Conservation in Third World National Parks**, in Bioscience 29(7): 414-418.

WTO/UNEP "Tourism Carrying Capacity". WTO/UNEP Joint Technical Report Series, 1992. Paris.

WTO. 1981. **Guidelines for the Use of National Resources in the Building and Maintenance of Tourist Plant**. World Tourism Organization. Madrid, Spain. 40 pp.

WTO. 1983. **Study on tourism's contribution to protecting the environment**. World Tourism Organization. Madrid, Spain. 26 pp.

WTO. 1983. **Risks of Saturation or Tourist Carrying Capacity overload in Holiday Destinations**. World Tourism Organization. Madrid, Spain. 41 pp.

WTO. 1985. **The Role of Recreation Management in the Development of Active Holidays and Special Interest Tourism and Consequent Enrichment of the Holiday Experience**. World Tourism Organization. Madrid, Spain. 28 pp.

WTO. 1985. **Identification and evaluation of existing and new factors and holiday and travel motivations influencing the pattern of present and potential domestic and international tourist demand**. World Tourism Organization. Madrid, Spain. 25 pp.

WTO. 1990. **Compendium of Tourism Statistics**. World Tourism Organization. Madrid, Spain. 265 pp. WTO. 1992.

WWF. 1990. **Ecotourism: The Potentials and Pitfalls**. (ed. E. Boo). Volumes 1 and 2. World Wildlife Fund. Washington, D.C. 274 pp.